1990

GETTING IT ON

GETTING IT ON

The Clothing of Rock 'n' Roll

BY MABLEN JONES

Ellen Colón-Lugo, costume consultant

ABBEVILLE PRESS

PUBLISHERS · NEW YORK

To Joseph Campbell,

whose volumes on mythology

have been a great influence on

and inspiration for

this book.

●

Library of Congress Cataloging-in-Publication Data
Jones, Mablen. Getting it on.
Bibliography: p. Includes index.
1. Rock musicians—Costume—History.
2. Rock music—History and criticism. I. Title.
GT6390.R63J66   1987   391′.04784   86-28869
ISBN 0-89659-686-9

Editor: Alan Axelrod

Art director: James Wageman

Designer: Jon Valk

Production supervisor: Hope Koturo

Text © 1987 by Mablen Jones

Compilation copyright © 1987 by Cross River Press, Ltd.

Jacket photo credits—front (l. to r.): Mark Weiss, Mark Weiss, Michael Putland/Retna, Ltd.; spine: Paul Natkin/Star File; back (l. to r.): Stephen Morley/ Retna, Ltd., Ken Kaminsky/Star File, David Redfern/Retna, Ltd. Frontispiece: Cyndi Lauper (Retna, Ltd.)

Printed in Japan.

Contents

Rock's Heroes and Goddesses

A MYTHOLOGY

ock 'n' roll stars look dangerous. These frenetic heroes and goddesses in costumes ranging from glamorous to grotesque assault high culture. Wearing flamboyant phantasms of sequins and glitter, swaggering studded skins of leather lusting for action, and tatters emblazoned with heraldic emblems of otherness, they exhibit a licentious mania for sybaritic visions and sounds. They express the romance of recklessness and the spectacle of excess at its outermost limits of agony and ecstasy. Shining skintight satins and Spandex, pimp-dapper sharkskin suits, gowns with holes, fringes, and safety pins, garish make-up, and tonsorial styling create libertine images that separate the modish from the mean, the simps from the wailing sirens.

Nikki Sixx of Motley Crüe, dressed by Fleur Thiemeyer, 1984

The raw power of rock stars lies not merely in the release of repressed desire, but also in the evocation of primordial images from the wellsprings of archetype. Clad in clinging shreds of a sequined sheath terminating in a raggy hem of fringed strips that spin out centrifugally, Tina Turner becomes the incarnation of the tribal Great Goddess who radiates luminous energy, enthralling all those who see her. When the bad boys in leather, from Gene Vincent and Link Wray through Jim Morrison of the Doors, Sid Vicious of the Sex Pistols, Rob Halford of Judas Priest, and Billy Idol, flaunt their lizardlike armor trimmed with metal symbols of their inescapable badness, they become the invincible Trickster of myth. The adventures of this collective "hero with a thousand faces" (as mythologist Joseph Campbell calls the archetype) serve to release the flow of life energy into the world. Its leather-clad contemporary

fictional counterparts have long peopled such comic strips as *Terry and the Pirates* and the comic-book series *Blackhawk*. The self-ravaging punk antihero cathartically and messianically vents collective rage within a tradition of ecstatic martyrdom as he is pelted onstage with assorted objects hurled by fans.

Rock superstars have taken on the role of sacred public magicians, both in costume image and performance. The hysteria common to their fans assumes qualities of possession and trance; with voracious hunger they collaborate in a rite, creating celebrities that are the romantic equivalent of the heroes of ancient myth and folk tales. These figures validate a belief that life can be glamorously magical, something beyond the deadening conformity of convention. Rock stars defy decorum. Their will is not that of official society, but that of the self, and such self-determination is seen as heroic. They offer images of libertinage even as they exalt monogamous love to an astral plane. The openly erotic costumes of many rock performers brazenly consummate fantastic yearnings for glamour, protesting any existence that lacks sensual excitement, and elevating both performer and fans far above the ordinary. The rock performer is the hero or goddess who would guide all into a realm of energy and delight, a cosmic dancer with comic spirit who transports the devotee into rapture.

The most dynamic and enduring rock stars have developed iconic costumes that clearly identify them as mythic characters who satisfy the psychic thirst for larger-than-life human symbols. Their cos-

*E*lvis Presley on a Harley, with unidentified starlet, 1957

tumes not only help fans enter a realm of wonder and catharsis, they similarly transform the performer into something other than his or her ordinary self. These outfits overcome inhibition by separating a stage role from the customary self-image to produce

*P*aul Stanley of Kiss, dressed by Fleur Thiemeyer, 1980–81

an altered state that permits extraordinary ways of acting. Legend has it that when David Bowie revealed why he made up so many costume characters early in his career, he claimed that they allowed him to perform his songs in a way that inhibition denied his ordinary self. Fantastic costume helps suspend

stage anxiety by letting "another" stand in for one's quotidian personality. Religion has always used costumes as transcendental devices in ritual, and, of course, all actors are aware of costume's potency.

Successful rock costume is a type of expressionistic caricature that eliminates all detail that does not contribute to a specific character. Fans must know instantly who are the bad boys and girls and who are the good. The garb not only visually reinforces the content of the songs but, like a successful cartoon, reveals character and predicts what action one might expect next. (Indeed, top rock costume designers like Bob Mackie, Fleur Thiemeyer, and Betsey Johnson often use cartoonlike sketches to design outfits.) Part of the tension of a rock act is the expectation and anticipation of violence or prank, the waiting for the peroxide-Mohawk-tressed, studded-leather-bikini-and-chaps-clad Wendy O. Williams of the Plasmatics to destroy any object in sight. As with satirical caricature, rock costume distorts the norm as a stance of opposition, exaggerating forms and silhouette in an act of conscious fancy.

*B*ob Mackie sketch of a gown for Tina Turner

*T*ina Turner, 1973

What visually establishes stars as rebels is a ruthless abrogation of good taste. They demonstrate opposition to normality and decorum by accentuating voluptuous and vulgar elements. If understatement represents a tenet of fashionable elegance, rockers multiply their jewelry and exaggerate their hairstyles to baroque excess. When beige cashmere pleated skirts and slacks are the cool conservative look, rockers adopt hot tiger-striped Spandex as a second skin. If natural-shoulder and unstructured jackets are in vogue, the padded extravagance of shoulder extensions structure the hard-rock costume top. The oppositional stance of rock, like the satiric cartoon, violates normative clichés. Its arrogance proclaims the performer's superiority to fashion at the same time as it creates its own stereotypes of *clearly* extraordinary beings.

Yet it is important to realize that, even at its most outrageous, rock costume draws upon convention—historic traditions and those cultural motifs we call myths. For example, harshly contrasting dual or multicolor schemes descend from the medieval fools and Elizabethan clowns, who wore two-part and two-toned costumes to symbolize the rational versus irrational division of the mind. Purposefully cut holes and deliberate mixtures of styles worn in the medieval Feast of Fools, and the early harlequin costumes with irregular patches from the Italian commedia dell'arte preceded the regular-patterned outfit smoothly emblazoned with stylized diamond-shaped lozenges. Female rock harlequins in thrift-shop mix and mismatch have included Janis Joplin, Cyndi Lauper, and Madonna.

MYTH AND ARCHETYPE

For many people myth is ignorant superstition or tales for kids. Yet, since the eighteenth century, scholars have recognized myth as an unconscious, intuitive mode of thought that balances our rational intellectual mental states. Philosopher-critic Roland Barthes claimed that, today, a discontinuous image system has replaced the long-fixed mythical stores of classical heroes. For example, our astronaut figure—which Barthes calls the "jet-man," becomes an imaginative equivalent of the Grail-seeking Parsifal. Mythologist Joseph Campbell calls such images the guiding symbols of society. Without having been self-consciously invented, they arise, take form in the output of seers and artists of all kinds, and promote our sense of well-being. Every holiday and every historic hero is enhanced with mythic legend and imagery. This is not to say that myth is false in its embellishment of "reality," but only that it expresses psychic truths rather than veritable history. It truly reveals our fears, joys, fantasies, and desires. Myth is rooted in real experience, but it is guided by emotional rather than intellectual perceptions.

Unlike dream, myth is universal and cannot be private or singularly personal. Myth deals with types of exemplary models of ideal people—whether good or evil, since villains are just as mythic as the good guys. Myth is like a *shared* dream, which transforms singular situations and individual personalities into archetypes to which everybody can relate.

Archetypes include images from the reservoir of conscious cultural history as well as from what Carl Jung called our "collective unconscious." Theory also has it that the different archetypes portrayed by Greek mythology were originally all aspects of a single godhead—the great goddess predating all other religions throughout the world. When self-conscious reflection differentiated various aspects of nature, both good and evil, a whole hierarchal pantheon of gods and semidivine heroes appeared. The ancient hero and antihero, clowning trickster, androgyne, tempting siren, vampire, magical child, and Dionysian martyr survive in contemporary rock music character roles.

The Great Goddess stood for the totality of what could be known, while the male human hero sought knowledge by working for it through trial or quest. The mythic trickster, who lacked moral consciousness, became a vehicle of speculation on the problem of ethics. Shamans and other human incarnations of the impulse to self-determination have been associated with animal figures such as the raven, coyote, and Br'er Rabbit on up to the contemporary Daffy Duck, Bugs Bunny, and other comic cartoon animals. Performers like George Clinton and Grace Jones, who have used animal costume imagery, partake of this tradition that contains devils and prophets, demons and heroes, fire-bringers and temptor/temptresses. Their appeal is that they do what we cannot. They are collective alter egos.

Traditional myth-oriented societies possessed two types of semidivine heroes: the religious and the magical. Those of the first class were beings of a different order from humans and superior to them. These temporary divine incarnates became theocratic rulers. The other sort, the public magicians or shamans, possessed high degrees of temporary spiritual power, which most of their "audience" believed themselves capable of achieving as well, though on a smaller scale. The magical semidivinities were human mediums, through which the energy of their culture flowed. Many of them were humorous as well. Even in this century, some Native American and South Seas societies have fraternities of sacred clowns, who sing, dance, present sexual display, and ignore taboos. Comic Vedic shamans in Sri Lanka, Yakit, and Taosian Indian groups also identified with powers of archetypal gods and performed in sessions of spirit possession. Some presented dual opposing traits—manliness and effeminacy, humaness and beastliness, dexterity and clumsiness—and insisted on getting social custom all wrong. The medieval European jester, the wise fool dressed in coxcomb and motley asymmetry, who mocked any auspicious occasion, continued the tradition. Comic rockers like Screamin' Jay Hawkins, with his capes and coffins, and George Clinton, in animal costume or television-antenna-equipped football helmet, con-

tinue to ridicule convention. While the costumes of many performers may seem arbitrary, silly, or superficial, the most successful outfits touch emotions deeper than what is immediately apparent.

Although hard-rocking stars often seem to be the rebels, while MOR (middle of the road) and AOR (adult-oriented rock), or soft rock, appear to favor benign figures, even these glamorous costume characters often have a numinous power that transgresses common notions of reality. Michael Jackson, who once appealed primarily to black teens, crossed all ethnic barriers into the realm of mass appeal after he changed his face, hair, and costume to become a glittering androgyne. Even the middle-aged audience, who generally eschew rock, adored the bejeweled Elvis Presley in cartoonlike spacesuits with capes. Performers need not play rebel-with-or-without-a-cause to sell records, but they do need to transcend that which we usually are and appeal to mythic archetypes.

While Prometheus—the rebel and working-class rock hero—maintains his stature in work clothes, Aphrodite takes a step down to wear the same. Preservation of her numinousness requires dress that removes her from the realm of hard labor. Connie Francis, a good girl next door in shirtwaist dresses, embodied the pre-labor-force virgin archetype, and any abrasive or wanton behavior or dress would have damaged her mythic image. By contrast, passionate Janis Joplin, in psychedelic finery of furs, feathers, and faux jewels, possessed a tough earthy rebel image equally compelling in its anti-dress-for-success stance. But when Elvis moved up from working-class hero to become the King of Rock 'n' Roll, he had to trade in street clothes for sacramental glamour.

BECOMING AN ARCHETYPE

While a horse has to remain a horse all its life, and a cat must live as a mere feline, human beings can challenge a simple biological and environmental identity to become an artist, astronaut, warrior, or writer. Career roles may become what poet Robinson Jeffers called "visions that fool us out of our limits." Rock stars very often create their own rebirths to become different characters within a fictive realm. Robert Zimmerman became Bob Dylan, David Jones became David Bowie, Reginald Dwight became Elton John, and scores of other popular music performers have taken on new identity and appearance as they launch their careers. Of course, stage names are nothing new, and Hollywood film companies once regularly ran contests to name their new stars. However, except for professional wrestlers, few entertainers have adopted monikers with such dubious associations as the rock musicians: Johnny Rotten, Gary Glitter, Alvin Stardust, Billy Idol, Eddie Money. All of these names help establish the character as a type. The association-laden name, costume image, and appropriate behavior establish a context for the kinds of songs and style of delivery. Just as actors and actresses like Rock Hudson and Joan Crawford embodied earlier Hollywood types, rock performers established in popular imagination such types as the greaser, the flower child, and the punk. Not that these types weren't already there, but the musician heroes synthesized the styles into

concrete emblems that brought those images into sharp focus as badges of communal identity.

The point here is that the more the individual comes to resemble either Everyman or Everywoman in an enhanced form, or else a transcendent figure who is something wholly other, the greater the possibility for mythic success. These types come to represent a realm that is transpersonal, universal, and even transcendent in the eyes of fans. This is not to claim that the process has always been deliberately cultivated and calculated. Often performers have inadvertently created public types out of desperation for privacy, to shield themselves from the onslaught of probing fans and media reporters. The propagation of hero-makes-good stories in rock-star fanzines, films, and books, which relay the public images, also hastens the mythologizing process.

After becoming an archetype, the figure then becomes infinitely repeatable for each generation. This has shown itself in the constant revivals of rock acts from the 1950s and 1960s. When contemporary performers imitate the music and costume style of their legendary heroes, they detach themselves from the profane here-and-now to enter magically the eternal time of myth. If the performers last long enough to develop their own synthesis of past and contemporary elements so that they are perceived as new or original, they may continue to work within their archetype indefinitely; in fact, attempts to shift it may be opposed by fans. Nevertheless, they must provide fans with a feeling of the world of heroes being created afresh with each performance and not simply a nostalgic rehash. For example, in 1984 both Madonna, in psychedelic paisley jacket and miniskirt, and Cyndi Lauper, in thrift-shop conglomerates reminiscent of Janis Joplin, were perceived as totally new and not indebted to types of the 1960s.

The longing for a paradisiacal time seems to recur each decade, and contrasting good and evil types repeat endlessly with heroes from each camp simultaneouly idolized. For example, bad boys Elvis Presley, Gene Vincent, and Jerry Lee Lewis contrasted with the angelic Pat Boone, Everly Brothers, and Ricky Nelson. Hard-drinking, -drugging, and sloppy Janis Joplin was the foil to piercing, cerebral, and sophisticated Grace Slick, whose drugs of choice were psychedelic and thus mind-expanding or "good" to that generation. The Beatles counterpointed the Rolling Stones, Patti Smith against Blondie, Michael Jackson versus Prince, and so on.

Performers are permitted to pass through a succession of personae only after attaining mythic stature. Fans strenuously resist changes in their heroes, unless they have gone beyond the requirement for profane consistency and into superstardom. In this case, changes are seen as development, and the superstar can do no wrong. For example, although Bob Dylan was booed at the Newport Folk Festival in 1965 for changing from acoustic folk hero to electric rocker, and even a second time soon after that, by the third concert at Carnegie Hall a few months later he had arrived and was accepted as a bona-fide superstar. His future changes of image were commented upon but not condemned, and in time they even became expected.

*M*adonna, *The Virgin Tour, ca. 1985*

BOB LEAFE/STAR FILE

Neither myth nor rock 'n' roll has been monopolized by a single principal goddess or hero. Even in ancient pantheons, mythic figures always fade out eventually, get mixed up with others, or transform themselves into animals or astronomical constellations. Archetypes rotate constantly as the unconscious and collective zeitgeist anticipates changes to come. In art we demand and expect change by lauding the avant-garde. In life and in rock 'n' roll the metamorphosis of heroes and goddesses continues without our conscious choice.

THE ROMANCE OF ROCK COSTUME

Rock imagery can appropriate subjective associations more completely than theatrical costume, which is tied to a naturalistic or literary convention. Unlike theater outfits, which must be logically congruent with the dramatic unities of time, place, and story, rock costume can arbitrarily leap back centuries (as did the 1960s musicians Paul Revere and the Raiders, garbed in ersatz American Revolutionary War uniforms), or go forward (as with Kiss's and LaBelle's science fiction outfits), or be completely wacky (like George Clinton and the Funkadelics). Although modern dance costume enjoys similar freedom to indulge in fantasy—and dance also has links with religious celebration—rock is closer to popular emotion than art and expresses itself with the fewest scruples of intellect and taste. Of all the popular expressive media, it most openly reveals collective fears, hopes, and passions. These costumes of romance and sorcery defy mortality by leaping among past, present, and future. They help summon the sphere of bliss and energy.

The image of the untamed and unrefined calls up visions of primal freedom and elemental forces, a golden age of libertinage without the tears and complications of civilization. Like splendid church vestments, glitzy, fantastic, or awe-inspiring glamour costumes open receptivity to feelings of revelation. Both extremes of costume—the rough and the glamorous—partake of the romance of raising the mundane to the sublime.

The essence of popular music, and especially rock 'n' roll, is romance, the repudiation of the secular banalities of life. Contemporary rock-music video, which also regularly uses cartoon animations and extravagant multimedia effects, sets a high register of intensity for impressionistic daydreaming. More than ever before, rock 'n' roll becomes the anthem of romance, and its costumes the mirror of its passions and desires.

Once, rock performers were simply thought of as entertainers. But within this decade rock stars have not only achieved the power and respect formerly accorded only to leaders in politics and the fine arts, they also became heroic representatives for those lacking Establishment voices: youth, minorities, and women. Their involvement with philanthropic causes, such as the concerts for "Live Aid" to benefit those stricken by famine in Africa and "Farm Aid" to help farmers and farm workers, won increased admiration for rock stars as caring human beings. The rockers emerged as idealists who have stepped in to try to salvage what politicians and bureaucrats have hopelessly botched up. Now they've emerged as *actual* heroes, whether or not their efforts achieve such lofty goals. Rock stars have become role models, not merely for fantasy but also for life.

Although few can copy what they do on the stage, all can emulate, to some degree, how they look. Indeed, their outfits have influenced the course of fashion. Our infatuation with rock-costume style as a means of personal expression celebrates theatricality as a legitimate way of being in the everyday world. This fluid concept of self transcends class: it is a notion of unlimited human potential for changing into anybody else, even a rock star. Their costumes are not merely changing the look of what we wear, but also our notions of freedom and fulfillment.

Anthropologists have proposed that there are at least two major cultures within each society: one authorized by ideal aesthetics and laws, and another, unconscious version, which is expressed in products and practices that the official culture would like to ignore or suppress. Most of this second, vulgar (from *vulgare*, or common people) realm is transmitted through popular images, for pictures are more compelling than words for instantaneous transmission. The working-class rock titan cannot represent the archetype in clothes that say elitist culture. If such a performer wants to transcend the up-from-the-ghetto look, she or he has to go for super glamour or else be outrageously "bad." A bit of divinity resides in the coarse and unrefined trick-ster. The powerful shaman and wise fool wore motley and mismatched outfits; with garb of increased taste and gentility, the shaman lost his former extrasensory aura and became a mere entertainer.

Authentic artists are also expected to cut through the veneer of cultivated convention. When Tina Turner introduced her 1970s version of the late-1960s Creedence Clearwater song "Proud Mary," she told us that she was not going to take it "nice and easy—because we do things nice and rough." Fans could anticipate ecstasy from Turner, arrayed in a Bob Mackie extravaganza of glitter and fringe with pleated wings in back and a décolletage down past her navel. None could mistake her for anything other than a fantastic erotic being from another world.

Romance in revolt from reality returns again and again in literature of all types, in works of Emily Brontë and Charles Dickens, in American fiction from Hawthorne and Poe to Faulkner and Pynchon as well as in contemporary mysteries, science fiction, and popular music. Hollywood films, famous from the 1920s through the early 1940s for their ability to triumph over reality, offered the intoxicating mythologies of screen goddesses. But when film degraded the divine fantastic into the naturalistic profane, only animated cartoons and Broadway musicals remained completely subversive of realist aesthetics.

Fitting the Costume to the Music

For over two decades American record companies believed that rock music did not sell on television. They applied cabaret, music hall, and theatrical costuming and visual techniques to the video medium, which requires different staging procedures and imagery. Embalming performers in the static studio proscenium setup—sometimes without live audience—was enervating to all but the most charismatic rockers. Today, in contrast, "abstract concept" videos with animation techniques and surreal montage clips have released music and image from the restraints of naturalistic narration. A high degree of fantasy has become the norm. Costumes have evolved to accommodate evolving styles of presentation.

Cher, dressed by Bob Mackie, late 1970s

In the beginning, rock 'n' roll music had none of its own clothes. Nineteen-fifties and early sixties rock was primarily an aural experience, despite its exposure in Hollywood films, live performances, and on television; for the dominant media of transmission were radio and records. When ordinary clothes were not worn, performance costumes were generally inspired by either of two traditions: the exaggerated stylization of professional gospel and stage vaudeville and the intimate cabaret styles of local bars. Among black pre-rock, rhythm-and-blues originators, male "criers" and "shouters" heightened their hyperbolic gyrations with close-fitting José Greco-type outfits. Women blues artists, who restricted their motions to hand gestures and tiny steps, wore lamé and spangled floor-length sheath gowns. But the majority of male blues stars, such as Muddy Waters, Howlin' Wolf, B. B. King, and Ray Charles, who achieved great popularity, and who were idolized by rock musicians, wore elegantly cut suits, ties, and white shirts. The impeccable ensemble signaled consummate professionalism and controlled artistry.

Young, poor white rockabillies of the mid fifties popularized two diametrically opposed looks: trashy and conservative. The first made the most out of bad-boy retail options, the clothes worn by black pimps, the other followed in the sport jacket or suit of country-western music, which was discarding the cowboy image at that time. A naturalistic approach was to persist among most white rock performers into the mid sixties. For the most part, during the early years, ambitious performers attempted to make themselves cleanly acceptable to the middle class for album cover photographs and cameo appearances on television variety shows and on Dick Clark's "American Bandstand" in order to placate parents, religious leaders, and public officials calling for the ban of rock 'n' roll. The very few female rock singers of that era all looked like they were either going to a chaperoned party or to the senior prom. The clothing camouflaged the musical message that was outraging adults. The message was sex.

There was no such thing as a costume designer for white rock singers. Most of the outfits were "pulled" pieces, brought from home and bought in neighborhood stores. Black artists, especially in groups, more often wore "built" outfits, costumes custom-made. The visual excesses of professional gospel troupes, who missed no opportunity to save souls with costume as well as music, were a union of visual and aural exaltation. Although Little

Richard brought it across ethnic lines in the fifties, and while it has been noted that Elvis Presley was inspired by gospel costumes, the style was not immediately influential with white performers until much later, when frequent arena performance created the necessity for outfits that read at great distances.

For the rock 'n' roll audience of the fifties, Hollywood films first established the American image of the young male as angry rebel more powerfully than did the musicians themselves. Even films that had nothing to do with music became wedded to rockers by association of youth with revolt. Marlon Brando in *The Wild One* of 1953, predating the popularization of rock music by a year, defined teenage antagonism to convention when he replied to heroine Mary Murphy's question, "What're you rebelling against?" with "Whatta ya got?" And that reply found its visual equivalent in Brando's leather jacket, jeans, and motorcycle boots. (The film was banned in Britain until 1967.) James Dean, in the 1955 *Rebel Without a Cause*, never wore leather at all, but his t-shirt and tight jeans came to symbolize the sensitive, misunderstood, and alienated youth driven against adult authority by inarticulate but "profound" urges. *Blackboard Jungle*, also from 1955, finally cemented the rock sound to juvenile delinquency by its use of Bill Haley and the Comets' song "Rock Around the Clock" on its sound track. It mattered not at all that Haley and his group were middle-aged ex-country-and-western musicians known to wear plaid sport jackets with ties and white shirts. The 1956 fictional film story of the music industry, *The Girl Can't Help It*, had shown

Little Richard, Gene Vincent, Eddie Cochran, and the Platters in actual performance. That image gave little offense in comparison to the power of bad-boy symbolism that Hollywood films generated.

Only later was the public offended by rockers' real-life actions. Elvis flaunted conventional taste only while supposedly possessed by the compulsion of the music. When the fit wasn't on him, he professed love of mother, country, and God. Not until the sixties did rock rebels deliberately and outrageously set out to become outlaws, both politically and aesthetically, when they stood for peace during the Vietnam War and for unlimited freedom with drugs, sex, and dress. The let-it-all-hang-out stance reached a peak of informality in the psychedelic era, when stoned acid- and folk-rock bands might appear in concert in anything they happened to find themselves in that morning, usually well-worn jeans, tie-dyed t-shirts, and boots.

Meanwhile, Hollywood films continued to develop another pole of the mythic rock hero. In addition to the dark bad boy, the films exploited an image of the good, light-hearted, fun-seeking sunshine spreader. *Jailhouse Rock* of 1957, portraying Elvis as a violent young rockabilly singer, and *High School Confidential* (for which Jerry Lee Lewis sang the title song) of 1958, about a teenage drug ring, were devoted to the bad-boy category. The opposing camp followed with such examples as *Don't Knock the Twist* in 1962, starring Chubby Checker, plus the numerous beach-blanket bonbons of Frankie Avalon and Annette Funicello, among them the 1963 *Beach Party*, 1965 *Beach Blanket Bingo*, and 1965 *How to Stuff a Wild Bikini*.

Walt Disney not only supervised Funicello's costumes on film but also her dress in daily life. In order to maintain the wholesome Disney image, she was instructed never to wear low-cut dresses. Well before 1960s Motown control of artists' costumes and public behavior, this was a forecast of the managerial direction that would later become more prominent. Indeed, Disney influence extends into the

Vic Morrow and Glenn Ford in The Blackboard Jungle, *1955*

eighties, as music television videos use his techniques of cartoon animation to create the magnetic appeal of joy in pure movement fused with sound. Even David Bowie's 1986 puppet-animation musical film, *Labyrinth*, contains echoes of Annette Funicello and fellow Mouseketeers singing in "The Mickey Mouse Club." It's possible that Disney's mythic and folkloric themes as well as his marriage of sound to form and abstract movement will provide further avenues for the surreal and fantastic in rock costume and imagery.

While Hollywood writers developed the mythic hero and delinquent roles, the film costume designers clothed singers as these characters and later created outfits for performing on stage and television. Designer Bob Mackie, who began working in film costume, brought glamour to rock 'n' roll through creations for Cher that spanned her 1970s television series. Each week audiences waited for the newest witty extravagance in cloth to appear on the most-photographed female singer of the decade. Although not a hard rocker, Cher was every inch the personification of the Great Goddess who took on many forms. Because of her exotic look, she hardly had to *do* anything—just pose in Mackie's outfits and sing a bit. Her face was that of every ideal female: she could look American, Italian, Jewish, American Indian, or a little of them all. Cher wore every kind of Mackie outfit, from that of a Follies showgirl, to Amazon or Aztec princess in feathers, beads, and oversized headdresses. The inspiration for several of Mackie's Indian outfits for Cher has been traced to John Harkrider's 1929–30 film designs, especially in the use of sequins and feathers; however, the costumes took on new meaning during the psychedelic era, which celebrated the Native American as a rock tribal emblem. Cher wore some of Mackie's outfits off-stage as well as on, turning every public appearance into a modeling session joyously received by every press photographer. Mackie's infamous 1974 "nude" gown for Cher, an absolutely sheer creation of nylon chiffon with bugle beads and nuggets sewn into strategic locations, made the covers of both *Vogue* and *Time*. Whatever inspiration it might have received from Marilyn Monroe's sequined sheath in *Some Like It Hot*, the illusion of beaded nudity was accomplished with such exquisite refinement that it made the dress Mackie's own.

His work set the standards for rock costumers of the eighties, who had to work for camera as well as stage performance. Whereas stage designers have realized the necessity for larger-than-life exaggeration, stylization, clear silhouette, reflectivity, and striking contrasts of dark and light, the close-up lens demands something else. It revels in texture, decorative patterning, detail, and subtle construction. It also mercilessly picks out bust padding, seams, and sweat lines in unlined outfits. Beading and sequins camouflage what is underneath as well as delighting the eye, but they can add the illusion of extra body weight if worked all over the outfit so closely as to give a solid texture without any smooth intervals. Mackie's combinations and contrasts of flesh and feathers, reflectivity, humor, and all-out fantasy gave rock costume mythic resonance by creating a contemporary image for the primeval goddess, who now happened to be doing rock 'n' roll.

After Mackie designed for the Supremes and Temptations on the 1968 television special *Taking Care of Business*, Diana Ross returned to him when she was out on her own doing night-club work. Mackie structured his visual effects very carefully. For example, in creating the opening costume for a certain song, Mackie needed to know just how Ross was going to move. The next piece would either build on the first or be completely different from it.

Cher, dressed by Bob Mackie: late 1970s; 1974 sketch; and 1986 Academy Awards

22

Cher

Bob Mackie

"After something completely wacky and outrageous, then you do a plain black sexy dress, and then the next one may be based on a leotard," Mackie says. When Diana Ross tried to switch things around, wearing the finale costume first and something like an in-betweener at the end, nothing worked.

When Mackie dresses a straight rock 'n' roll

appearance in Australia to arena rock 'n' rolling in New York. The archetypes range from devil to angel, magician to vizier, harlequin to formal artist in beaded tuxedo. All are combinations of jacket and pants or jumpsuit, so that the performer can get a new look onstage without making a pit stop for re-dressing. In tours like John's, the singer is respon-

*B*ob Mackie

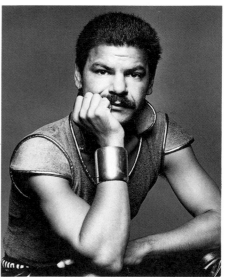

*L*arry LeGaspi

act in contrast to a night-club appearance, he does not try to structure it progressively. For Elton John's 1986 world tour, he built ensembles with layers that could be peeled off and intermixed according to Mr. John's needs. A problem with road tour dressing is that individual pieces may get destroyed; the rest of the parts must be able to succeed without them. Elton John chose fourteen out of fifteen colored sketches that offered a variety of looks for different occasions and countries, from a formal orchestra

*P*atti LaBelle, dressed by Larry LeGaspi, ca. 1972

sible for his jewelry and other accessories and chooses the order of outfits for each show. Mackie says that because he sees Elton John as something of a Dickens character, he also often uses period touches: "I used less this time, except for the derbies and skulky robes with the vests. Elton seems to be a romantic with a little bit of a sense of mischief."

Asked if he felt that there were any universal costume qualities that everyone responds to, Mackie replied: "It's usually something that doesn't look like you. They look at it and go 'Who's that?'"

*E*lton John, *dressed by Bob Mackie, 1986 tour*

While Bob Mackie brought glamour to American rock in the seventies, Larry LeGaspi made it respectable for hard-rocking males as well as the women. Although glitter rockers had been in drag since David Bowie's success in 1972, young American males had little sympathy for it. They wanted stars to look like stars, but neither like refugees from the backwoods nor campy London–New York decadents. The heavy metal band Kiss wore LeGaspi's famous outfits for ten years onstage and for all public appearances. In their costumes, LeGaspi created a unique hybrid archetype: a futuristic spaceman combined with animal imagery. The ancient belief in beings from other planets com-

bined with the modern astronaut to create the Adam of the future and was in turn fused with beastly incarnations of the mythic trickster shaman. The hybrid proved to have universal appeal. Moreover, as a complete disguise, it offered the wearers freedom to lead relatively normal lives off-stage; no one could recognize them out of costume. In addition to maintaining his own clothing retail outlets and designing a line of fashion, LeGaspi also worked with LaBelle from 1972 to 1982, Grace Jones and George Clinton and the Funkadelics in 1977.

Although Kiss's image was the one that became most famous, LeGaspi had evolved its basics in 1972 with Patti LaBelle's group. As a student, he

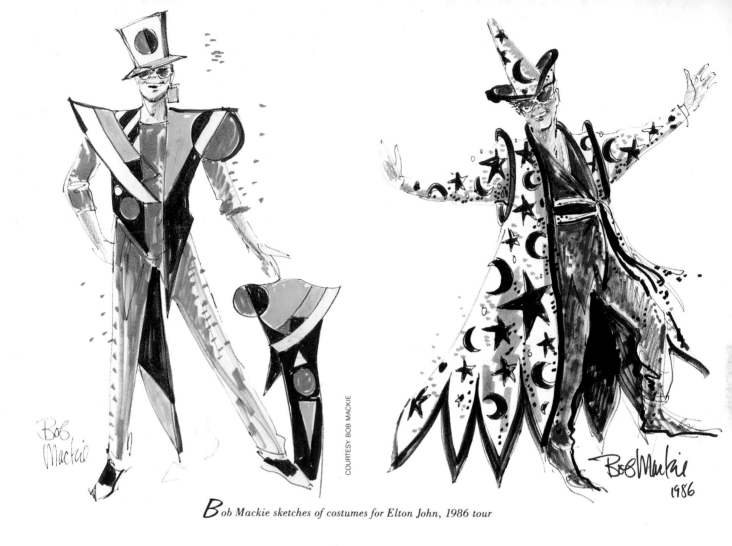

*B*ob Mackie sketches of costumes for Elton John, 1986 tour

had been a fan who went to all their shows and finally spoke with them after a performance.

They were just doing their metamorphosis from Patti LaBelle and the Bluebells to LaBelle, and they needed an image. I talked to them one night after a show and told them that I was into costume design and could do something for them. It all happened from that point on. . . . They were very courageous, for I was just learning to sew. My technical background was very limited. I had one semester of pattern-making and one semester of sewing and was taking illustration for a while. I quit F.I.T. [Fashion Institute of Technology] and opened a store with three dresses on the rack and one month's rent.

The futurist image for LaBelle evolved slowly over a year, beginning with a funkier look

that embodied some African feeling until group member Nona Hendryx said that she wanted a space suit. LeGaspi did one, and the rest of the group wanted it, too. They gave him full freedom to develop the image. He recounted the process:

I cut the pattern out like free-form sculpture because I had no idea what I was doing. I was going along with it, and the reason I came out with so many unusual shapes was that, once I would start twisting and playing with it, it became a free form. The trapunto pieces in nylon tricot plated with silver were made with cords sewn into the fabric one at a time.

He worked closely with each woman to differentiate their stage characters (this was no longer the clone

*S*ara Dash of LaBelle in a sterling-silver costume
by Larry LeGaspi and Richard Erker, ca. 1973

and Nona strained the garments to the breaking point—even with Spandex and extra tape and stitching in stressed areas. LeGaspi found that upholstery and padding were the only things Patti couldn't destroy.

Meanwhile, in 1973, LeGaspi's spacey outfits hanging in his Greenwich Village store attracted interesting customers—aliens and rock stars.

The funniest thing was that I actually had a woman, one of those people who actually thought they were an alien from outerspace, and a man and his wife who looked like they just came off of a tractor. They came into Moonstone and ordered space suits because they were going to stay out in the desert to wait for a spaceship to land. It was cash, and I made up three space suits for them. One of the women must have been eighty-five years old.

Much more famous customers were four young rock musicians who came into Moonstone looking for stage costumes to work with their already-designed Kabuki-style make-up. The original members of Kiss each had a distinct facial creation for their image: Peter Criss was the cat, Ace Freeley the starchild, Paul Stanley the beautiful androgyne, and Gene Simmons the demon. LeGaspi recalls that it was very easy to work something up since they already had a definite look and direction. He spoke with great enthusiasm about the freedom and rewards of working with rock musicians—as opposed, say, to torch singers, who are very controlled.

When a performer breathes life into the clothing, that's where you get off as a designer. Not until it actually goes onstage, when the lights come up as they walk out, and the audience responds to it do you get that feeling. At retail it's a dress, but this is an image.

era of the sixties). Although the costumes were not *verbally* planned out in advance, they developed as the performers told him what they were most comfortable in. Nona Hendryx became very androgynous; Sara Dash was very sexy and wanted minimal clothing; Patti LaBelle covered up as a kind of emissary, a leader. Sara moved the least, while Patti

I look at these photos [costumes for LaBelle] and think of the work and hours. These were a labor of love at the time. They really were. These outfits will probably never be duplicated because no one would be stupid enough to sit down and spend 300 hours on them. But it was great because you felt that you were helping someone who had something and were making it a bit more. When they walked onto the stage and people would scream and yell because they looked so incredible, that's when you felt the rush. It always felt great.

Although the designer has not sought out other rock performers and has continued to go his own way with glamorous clothing design, mainstream rock artists have continued to buy his eighties garments to wear both onstage and off. Whitney Houston and Dionne Warwick have purchased his work from specialty stores.

Music video, which inundated most American television channels during the eighties, has profoundly changed the approach to rock dressing. When image almost more than sound became a badge of identity, music management often demanded that musicians stay with one look for a fixed period and then carefully change it a bit while retaining a basic style. Costume specialization in different types of rock outfits (for example, heavy metal as opposed to country-and-western-influenced rockabilly) became common, and the business became much more exacting and subject to high-pressure deadlines. No longer did designers have the leisure to experiment with alternatives. The design had to convey a very specific image, be made in no time flat, wear like Kryptonite, move

*P*atti LaBelle, ca. 1973

like water, and photograph like the finest gossamer silk, luxurious satin, or supple leather.

Fleur Thiemeyer has emerged as one of the front-runners of eighties rock dressing with her work for Motley Crüe, the new Kiss, Heart, Lover Boy, Pointer Sisters, Pat Benatar, Rod Stewart, Journey, Ozzy Osbourne, the Jacksons, and dozens of others. She claims that the rock costume explosion has been as big a surprise to her as to anyone else, that ten years ago she didn't believe she could make a living, much less a big business, out of dressing rock 'n' roll bands. Now she not only designs their clothes, but also the total image—everything visual in set-ups for the album cover, the video, stage and public appearances, as well as press photographs. "When I take on a project, it's the nails, the make-up, the hair, what shoes you're going to wear, what

*S*cience-fiction fantasies by Larry LeGaspi

your weight-loss capacity is, putting trainers with you. It's absolutely the whole concept." When she works with performers who have already trained themselves through long experience, she gives them exactly what they want—but with more flamboyance and flash than even they might have conceived.

Like Larry LeGaspi, Fleur Thiemeyer came to rock dressing through a love of the music itself. As a teenager in Australia she went to the music clubs and became friends with the musicians. When

a girlfriend who was making clothes for bands asked Fleur to help her with the sewing, she had no intention of becoming a designer and was offered a scholarship in athletics at a university. However, there were few employment opportunities for her, and the only wage she could have made as a student was between thirty and forty dollars a week. Having learned to sew from her mother, a home economics teacher, and possessing the artistic eye of her father, a former commercial artist, she discovered that she

ILLUSTRATOR: KARL KOFED COURTESY LARRY LEGASPI

could make three pairs of pants in a day and sell them for ten dollars each. To save money to go abroad, she also worked as kitchen help in some discotheques and briefly modeled.

When she came to America she answered two advertisements on the backs of fashion magazines: one for the Fashion Institute of Design in Los Angeles and another for an interior decorating school. The Fashion Institute not only accepted her first, they eventually presented her with the Bob

Mackie Design Award and introduced her to Mr. Mackie. Even before she completed two years of class at the Institute, she helped costume three of Dick Clark's rock 'n' roll road shows and did some Las Vegas dressing for Olivia Newton John and Helen Reddy. She went to school mornings and worked for Bill Whitten in the afternoons, helping with outfits for Elton John, Earth Wind and Fire, and the Edgar Winter Group. "Then it really clicked with me," she recalled. "I don't think that I had taken getting into costuming quite seriously until being around it in that environment and doing chain-mail suits for Steppenwolf and the bands of

*F*leur Thiemeyer

the late sixties." She began doing all of Olivia Newton John's costumes herself and toured with her. "And then I met up with Rod Stewart, and it just

happened." Each client recommended her to others, her work was admired, and her reputation grew.

However, costuming was becoming increasingly controlled by outside forces. After public outrages over the heavy metal, glitter, and punk rock of the seventies, television censors, by 1982, were refusing to air videos they found excessively obnoxious. Moreover, towns and arenas were barring hard-rock bands, and parents were preventing their children from attending certain concerts. In order for many musicians even to be heard, their images had to pass muster by self-policing media executives as well as by self-appointed public arbiters.

It became a greater challenge to create a dynamic, singularly definitive image for each band amid the fierce competition and restrictions. Furthermore, in instances where one set of costumes had been fixed on as the signature look, it had to be made to work for all media—be theatrically larger than life for stage and yet have rich enough texture and detailing for video and photographic close-ups. Whereas black leather used to be the staple for bad boys and girls, it doesn't take advantage of the multicolored stage lights and makes performers look smaller in arenas. Color and flowing fabrics enhance the sweep of broad gestures.

Fleur Thiemeyer became known not only for her use of dazzling color combinations but also for outfits that looked as animated in the steady close-up as in whirling motion. She says she prefers that her costumes be seen in action, when you can't detect every sequin and nail head. They become apparitions of pure energy and delight. Because they are hard-working outfits that must withstand extraordinary wear, as well as be compatible with a musician's own feelings about him- or herself, Thiemeyer extensively interviews her clients, finds out how they move, and gives them amplifications of their own self-images. She even gave members of the new Kiss black-and-white copies of costume sketches and colored pencils, and she asked them to fill in the hues.

Sometimes the musicians are so preoccupied with finishing their album recording sessions before a tour that they don't give any thought to what they want to wear onstage. Thiemeyer determines how long they are going to keep pieces on and if they are likely to throw half of their wardrobe off in two or three songs (she adds flamboyant linings to jackets that are stripped off and whirled around), the temperature of the performing locations (Osbourne performed in Rio de Janeiro, where heat necessitated light dressing), and how many changes they would like to make during a show. After the consultation, measuring, and approval of sketches, she makes up three major outfits in an interchangeable systematized wardrobe that might break down into fourteen combinations of pieces in a layering format. The performers play around with the parts while on the road to find out which ones they tend to wear most often and which they want changed or elaborated upon, and then they send orders back to her for more. Another reason for starting a tour with a limited supply is that many musicians have a few inches to get rid of after months of comfortable home life. She starts them with garments with a little give,

*R*od Stewart, dressed by Fleur Thiemeyer, 1980s

and in about three weeks sends out pants a good inch-and-a-half smaller. Moreover, the bands need different costumes according to the country and size of arena they are playing in. Thiemeyer claims that even though Ozzy Osbourne is a god of heavy metal in England, he can't wear Thiemeyer's most bizarre outfits there because the kids just don't understand or appreciate them. Not only are the ones designed for 150,000-seat arenas too flamboyant for most of the smaller, 5,000-capacity British and European auditoriums, the teens want more straight machismo (what they're used to from the band AC/DC). The extreme forms of British rock dressing, such as what the Eurythmics, Culture Club, or Thompson Twins wear, are detailed fashion statements attuned to close viewing in clubs or video.

Whereas Bob Mackie originally worked with women and in an era when these females moved in stylized and controlled dance steps, the majority of Fleur Thiemeyer's customers are men, many of whose rambunctious exertions onstage leave the costumes dripping with sweat and in need of laundering. The fine silks of Hollywood legend have given way to tough synthetics that are all hand washable. Experience has taught that if dry cleaning doesn't destroy the beading and other decorations, it permanently embeds perspiration into the fabric and ruins it. Even Ozzy Osbourne's fifteen-pound vermicelli-beaded nylon-chiffon robe of 1985 is completely washable. Thiemeyer also eliminates inner linings for men's outfits, so that the wardrobe people can easily get to and repair torn seams. The

*O*zzy Osbourne, dressed by Fleur Thiemeyer, 1986

audience doesn't mind wet sweat areas and lines on the torsos of male outfits the way they do on those for females. Glamour, practicality, movement, photogenic appeal, plus a unique image for each band are the dressing prerequisites of Thiemeyer's clients. Her work fulfills not only their needs but also generates an enthusiasm and energy in the designer, who appears to love every minute of what she does.

By the mid eighties, rock music performance became so intertwined with special effects and media collages from film and electronic graphics

that naturalistic limitations on costumes began dropping away. The newest groups, without access to such resources, usually build their following in nightclubs. "Pulled" rather than "built" outfits predominate because they are inexpensively available in used clothing stores and flea markets. Musicians, more visually aware today than in any other decade, personalize outfits by recombining, painting, or

*P*at Benatar, dressed by Fleur Thiemeyer, 1984

adding to the pieces in some way. Notwithstanding what is being shown on music television, the coming trends have most often risen from the street rather than descended from the top of the corporate ladder. Despite the apparent big-business takeover of rock performance and its imagery, the romance of rock 'n' roll resides in the fact that rebellious and creative *individuals* can still turn the look and music around. That is what has happened over and over throughout rock history.

The Originators

*T*he 1950s were rock's Golden Age, the mythic Eden of innocence and exuberance, when the music recreated the world for youth and set styles of costume that persist today, both for performers and youthful fans. No matter that history recounts devastating personal and political repression of minorities and women. Post-war rock fans remember the birth of rock music rather than the ominous 1951 establishment of the Central Intelligence Agency, U.S. spy flights intensifying the Cold War, the 1954 Nixon "Checkers" speech defending fraud for personal gain, that same year's explosion of hydrogen bombs by both the U.S. and U.S.S.R., and the brutal crushing of the Hungarian revolt. Instead, rock memory focuses on the utopian atmosphere, the prosperity that brought

*E*lvis Presley, *dressed by Bill Belew, 1972*

cars (one to every three Americans) and seventy-two million telephones (more than half of the world's total was in the U.S.A.). *Life* magazine popularly acknowledged abstract art in an article on Jackson Pollock; and Marilyn Monroe, Brigitte Bardot, John Wayne, and Fess Parker (as Davy Crockett) were film or television idols. For rock music fans it was the decade when the goodness of youth and its music triumphed over the evils of adult hypocrisy.

Perhaps the event that did the most to spread the Edenic spirit was the entry of television into fifty million U.S. homes. It brought the fantasy of animated cartoons, science fiction, situation comedies, and the newest music, as well as the news. What previously took years to spread in popularity from one region or country to another, now flashed across the nation, turning us into a mass culture in a way that even radio had not. All could see new styles of being, looking, and acting; moreover, all could experience immediately the evolving youth culture. In the late 1940s, F.B.I. director J. Edgar Hoover warned of catastrophe at the hands of lawless teens: "like the sulphurous lava which boils beneath the slumbering volcano—such is the status of crime in America today." The teen even briefly displaced the Communist as a suitable target for fear and loathing. Youth looked alien in their rock 'n' roll-influenced clothing and sounded ominous as they imitated their new heroes.

For many middle-class adults fearful of lower-class hostility, the image of early rock performers was linked with criminality. The menace of youthful masses in proletariat garb appalled not only well-to-do parents, but also those aspiring to escape the ghetto. However, in the late fifties, dread of adolescents turned to competition for their pocket money; the media, formerly accused of fomenting delinquency, helped spawn a generation of rock 'n' roll consumers. By this time, psychologists had explained away anger and rebellion as nothing less necessary to normal development in teenage years than toilet training was in infancy.

But the Establishment could neither suppress, diminish, nor explain away the power of the new mythology. Popular music heroes and goddesses differed from the old crooners by evoking a parable opposed to theirs. They not only waged war on adult taste, their performances transformed reality into a battle where "bad" was "good," where the rebel stood against adult corruption and compromise. Looking different was a way of being revolutionary for rock 'n' rollers, not in the obvious sense of de-

stroying institutions, as was at first feared, but in a more metaphorical manner—by creating popular symbols for a different life-style that was about to shatter conventional notions of sexuality.

On the other hand, it is true that such bad boys as Little Richard, Elvis Presley, Gene Vincent, Jerry Lee Lewis, and Chuck Berry may have also served to stimulate desire for counterparts on the "good" side. Figures such as Buddy Holly, the Everly Brothers, and Pat Boone heightened the romance of good and bad. The "good guys" assuaged panic at being swallowed up by the sheer instinct of the licentious pole of the dual archetype. Perhaps counterparts were even essential, enhancing each other's assets by contrast.

MYTH AND REBELLION

In early religious traditions, licentious appearance and behavior have been historically sanctioned on festive occasions. To encourage growth of buried seed, fertility cults of Fauna, celebrated by women in pre-Christian Rome at the beginning of December, featured drunken howling and lustful advances upon men. Saturnalia, the Roman festival in honor of Saturn, allowed unrestrained carousing, as did the tradition of carnival, which survives today in Mardi Gras.

Our cultural division between the sacred and secular realms, which had formerly been merged in ancient times, severed our participation in mythic rituals on a daily and seasonal basis.

When we lack such regular, mythically sanctioned festival outlets, our celebratory enthusiasms focus on figures who act out for us the gestures and costumes of impropriety. In return, we bestow upon these figures *stardom*, the divine qualities of celebrity that were at the heart of mythic communal rites. We also sacrifice and discard their images after having consumed as much of their performance as we need. As in pagan days, the good and evil heroes and goddesses die and are reborn each decade. What is new, perhaps, is that we package and sell the demonic through secular rather than established sacred channels.

Although we temporarily discarded our first round of rock heroes at the end of the fifties, we resurrected them just as the ancients regularly resuscitated their agricultural deities.

Elvis Presley made a comeback in 1968; after his death in 1977, more of his records were sold than when he was alive. By the seventies all the "sins" of rock's first gods had been forgiven, and they had passed into the pantheon of the mythic deities who periodically rise from the grave. While they lived and aged, they were simply working-class heroes. After death they were eligible for apotheosis.

THE BAD BOYS

Bad boys, who are really good under their rude exteriors, appear throughout myth. The Greek god Zeus, later known as the Roman Jupiter, ranks as just such a good-bad prototype. The son of Kronos (Saturn, to the Romans) and Rhea (the Asiatic Cybele or Roman Ops), Zeus dethroned his father, committed incest with his sisters, daughters, and aunts, attempted to ravish his mother, and debauched a great number of maids and wives. Seasonally reborn, he took on many shapes, even those of beasts. But he also instituted a new order of consciousness. His revolution against Kronos, or Saturn, ended the age of innocence. Although amorous and capricious, often lacking in dignity and real power, he also initiated a sense of the moral responsibility of the individual, ended human sacrifice, exalted legal justice, and raised monogamy to an astral plane. Not dissimilar are rock star philanderers, who exalt love of an individual and love of justice in the same lyric form. Zeus's mother, Rhea or Cybele, the all-powerful fertility goddess, bequeathed to him the virtues of sexual celebration. Our rock stars, aided by costume, do the same for us.

Rock 'n' roll inherited the ecstatic gospel fervor, married it to sexuality, and ended the public wish for chaste innocence in children. Rock is hot and sexy, vulgar, and wild. Traditionally, the performers who became most mythologized looked the part of the sexy archetype. Those who represented the "good" half of the dual deity probably sold more records during their active careers than later. While Pat Boone's covers (a "cover" is one artist's version of another's original record) at first outsold Fats Domino's and Little Richard's originals, making nasty black rock palatable to affluent whites, it's those "bad" originals we've ultimately canonized.

Rock images in song and performer appearances signaled a new style of romance freed from what the ancient Greeks personified as the goddess Ananke (from whom the word *anxiety* derives), encircling limits of necessity—specifically the limits posed by blues and country-western lyrics. Working-class and economically disadvantaged performers

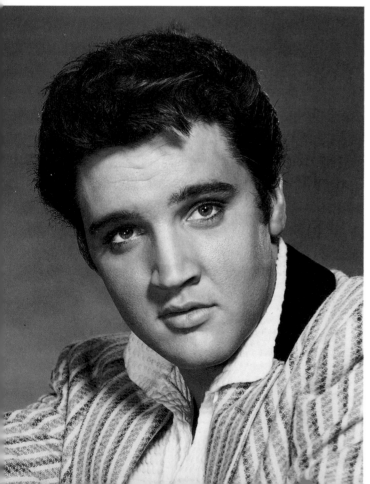

unknowingly combined classical mythology with that of rags-to-riches American folklore to create a new primeval reality, a narrative satisfying spiritual wants, moral cravings, and national beliefs. (One of the legends about America has been and still is the belief that a poor peasant immigrant can become the wealthy equivalent of royalty here and can find new friends and family to replace those people left behind in the Old Country.) Their fledgling myth was the creation of a rock community, a time of new beginnings, a belief in unlimited possibilities, and the creation of leaders who became larger than life by realizing a collective dream.

THE POTENCY OF ROCK COSTUME

The first people to make rocking sounds (such as The Mississippi-bred Graves Brothers' recording of "Barbecue Bust" and "Dangerous Woman" in the 1930s) are not the ones we raise from the dead. Figures who lacked the appearance of glamour or were too old ordinarily failed to supply public images youth could identify with. T.N.T. Brags, an accomplished rhythm-and-blues musician, was performing hot music in an energetic style, but did not possess the visual appeal of gorgeously coiffed and costumed Little Richard. T. Bone Walker, known for establishing a musical style in the 1930s and 1940s that many blues and lead rock guitarists would emulate, became less popular than the youthful, dapper Chuck Berry. Bill Haley may have been the first white man to score a national rock hit, with "Rock Around the Clock" in 1954, but, chubby and

The early pompadour - – Little Richard and Elvis Presley

middle-aged, he dressed himself and the Comets in outfits that reeked of conservative origins. Elvis, by contrast, not only had the musical goods, he strenuously cultivated his public persona, beginning from the time he was in high school. The rock figures of legend knew either instinctively or self-consciously that it wasn't just music they were selling. It was performance, a style of hedonism, and a celebration of sex appeal. That in itself is nothing new. Their combination of visual and musical elements was.

What mythologists call the numinous—that which evokes some aspect of divine power—distinguishes itself by appearing to be something "wholly other," something radically different from what we already know. Although musicologists can trace its origins, the rockabilly style of poor southern hillbillies was foreign to official culture of the 1950s. At that time fashion arbiters were praising Dior's "New Look" of French elegance, which translated into white teen middle-class cinch-belt waists with full skirts puffed out by crinoline petticoats. This style, in turn, gave way to the mid-fifties import of the European chemise, trapeze, and the old Chanel look—all decidedly unsexy. America's own fashion leader, designer Claire McCardell, stressed casual sportswear and easy loose-fit clothing suitable for entertaining, suburban barbecues, and active sports. Nothing could contrast more with such clothing than the most threatening images adopted by the bad-boy rockers: the greaser, the pimp, the vamp, and the lunatic, all developments of the first rockabilly incursions into official culture.

These outlaw representations hint at legendary parables rooted in history. The mob at the gates, the specter of social disintegration terrified upwardly aspiring parents. But public opposition to the perceived threat posed by rock music initiated three other folk legends for the rest of our population (then under twenty-five years old). First, for youth, the rockers were the mythic triumphant heroes; second, they would become the shapers of a benign rock community; and third, they would always be mockers of "rot at the top." By wearing rock clothes, one could signal identification with others who refused the smoothly complacent Hollywood-cum-Doris Day version of the American dream. One could return to the purity of the traditionally transcendental ideals of Thoreau's "Civil Disobedience," Whitman's poetic self, which wanted to embrace all people and experiences, and Emerson's self-reliant man. What is especially American is a belief that the inward potential is open-ended, unlimited. The poor and ignorant can achieve untold riches and power. Therein lay its arrogant attitude and appearance, which separates it from country and blues images. The new rockers would look like anything they wanted to because they were making up the rules.

THE LEADERS OF THE PACK

Although numerous historical contributors to both the musical and sartorial rock archetypes might be cited, perhaps the two biggest heroes to become myths in their own lifetimes were Little Richard and Elvis Presley. Of the two, Elvis had the advantage of dying while famous, so that posterity could aggrandize his persona unhampered by the human vul-

nerability of a living person. Although Little Richard's musical performance and costume images were perhaps more striking, his business management was never as sophisticated as that of Tom Parker, who packaged Elvis into a mass dream.

Little Richard was so far beyond the pale of white culture that it took two decades of rockers to reinterpret his image by bringing it back to America through England's glamour men of the 1970s. Today, it has entered white mainstream hard-rock heavy metal and is also reflected in the costumes of Prince. Richard Penniman was wacky "glam" before it was chic, gay before it was okay, and stage wild before that was *de rigueur* for rock performers. John Lennon claimed Little Richard and Elvis as his two great influences. James Brown, Chuck Berry, Otis Redding, Buddy Holly, Jimi Hendrix, and David Bowie all cited Little Richard as an inspiration.

Arrayed in his glittering suit of glass mirrors, Little Richard would mount the piano or speakers in mid song, while shafts of spotlights would focus on his incandescent striptease. His hair, piled into a preposterous pompadour or, later, teased into a bouffant, was usually processed a foot over his head. In 1954, on- or off-stage, his shirts were so loud that (according to his aide Bumps Blackwell) "it looked as though he had drunk raspberry juice, cherryade, malt, and greens and then thrown up all over himself. Man, he was a freak." Little Richard sought out quantities of different-colored glittery stones and sequins, capes, blouson shirts, pancake make-up, and mascara. For his

Little Richard, 1959 and 1970

cameo appearance in the Alan Freed film *Don't Knock the Rock*, Little Richard, sporting a baggy silver suit, for a pregnant interval posed motionless as a mannequin before his incendiary convulsion into motion and paroxysm of sound, "Awop-Bop-A-Loo-Mop-Alp-Bam-Boom," while thrashing the keyboard, flinging his long hair from side to side, and flailing his limbs. Elvis shook his pelvis, but Little Richard put everything into motion. He gained no

MICHAEL OCHS ARCHIVES, VENICE, CALIFORNIA

sense of decorum after his temporary retreat into gospel preaching. His British tour wardrobe in the mid seventies featured a parody of the royal image, with gaudy robes, heavy pancake make-up, and extravagant hairdos. Off-stage, at the Wembly Stadium press conference, he wore loud green pants with braces and a blouse with puffed-up sleeves. Although the "Teddy Boys" of 1975 jeered at the band's Afro wigs, Richard was in his glory with a plummeting v-neck pink jumpsuit and glitter collar.

KWAME BRATHWAITE/GREAT MOMENTS OF SOUL COLLECTION

How had he gotten away with it during the fifties? According to his autobiography: "We decided that my image should be crazy and way out so that adults would think I was harmless. I'd appear in one show dressed as the Queen of England and in the next as the Pope." He'd stand onstage and tell them how beautiful he was—then they'd agree with him. He had costumes for every night of an appearance and sometimes one for every song, with such pieces as a huge white satin cape with a red interior or a little red jacket with inch-square mirrors sewn all over. He claimed that they loved the outfits almost as much as they loved the show.

Little Richard used the costumes as disposable props as well as decorative garments. The striptease with which he concluded his act cost him thousands of dollars. He wore detachable pieces so that he could throw parts of the ensemble to the crowd, even his mirror-glass suits and shoes. He recalled that, "I was spending most of my money on costumes, then throwing them to the audience. . . . But it was worth it because everybody was talking about it and coming to see me do it." One outfit he wore during the late psychedelic years included a green fringed bolero top, beads, pants, and silver slippers. He'd start with the beads; then, removing his shoes, slowly tease the waving forest of audience arms. At the end, he slid off his fringed top and pretended to throw it out. When he finally flung it, the mob converged upon the prize, fighting and ripping it apart as Little Richard made his getaway from the house. This ritual recalled the orgiastic conclusion of the myth of Dionysus, in which the god is dismembered by the female Furies.

How did he come to dress this way?—by studying older professionals when he toured with black musical and comedy variety shows as a teenager. He reported that he admired the gospel-style blues shouter and crier Billy Wright, who performed around Atlanta. Wright sported very loud clothing with shoes to match, curled his hair, and wore make-up. Little Richard found out that he used "Pancake 31" and began applying it to himself. He also claimed that he designed some of the glass suits himself, but hired Melvyn James from Detroit and Tommy Rush from Los Angeles to make them. Little Richard recounted that he used a potato and lye hair-straightening concoction and hot combing curlers. He and other members of his band also changed clothes two or three times during a show because of "all the sweating" from dancing.

Screamin' Jay Hawkins may have been more exotic, but Richard played the beauty with good humor. Moreover, it was believed that black women could not resist the allure of processed hair, manicures, ruffled shirts, and florid or heavily styled jackets. Like the falsetto singing style that came directly from Africa, such trappings were perceived as the very essence of virile expression. If the "dandy" feeling of dress and walk was a distinctive black masculine style, the criteria of success for a blues crier-shouter was the intensity and conviction with which the song and image were carried off. And here Little Richard gained national notoriety. For a while, even disc jockeys attempted to gain credibility and empathy from white teens enamored of Little Richard and other shouter-singers by simulating their ravings, groans, and shouts.

The cry singer's stage techniques and use of costumes as props originated in inspirational rituals. The climax of the preacher's act came when he dropped to one knee, asking the audience "Did you eveh cry?" or some other question about suffering that could be responded to with an affirmative shout. Richard's variation was, "Aren't I beautiful?" and his lyrics stressed the hedonism of boy-meets-girl themes. Cry singers also appeared in José Greco outfits, and they peeled off jacket, tie, and sometimes even their shirts as their gyrations became more agitated. The strip, or "soul-baring," represented getting down to the nitty-gritty. Following Little Richard, James Brown enlarged the knee-drop dramatically, while, later still, Prince, in his 1986 video "Kiss," discarded his designer jacket and bright cropped-top bolero shirt to perform most of the song in the traditional falsetto-voice delivery, in his tight pants and high-heeled boots.

What helped make Little Richard a rock 'n' roll star was that he took the pain out of rhythm and blues and transcended the pedestrian slice-of-reality country-and-western trap in favor of transpersonal—as opposed to autobiographical—fantasy and fun. A combination of rascal and clown, he was the traditional harlequin, the trickster or jester of carnival and royal court. Unfortunately, some of his costume heirs in the late seventies and eighties diminished the cosmic aspects, taking themselves quite seriously; and they have compromised Richard's powerful rawness by adopting clothing styles of glamour more akin to establishment taste than parody of it. Some heavy metal glitter is more beautiful than provocative.

Screamin' Jay Hawkins, another crier-shouter and rock-image pioneer, lacked the glamour of Little Richard, but did prefigure the ghoul school of Alice Cooper's shock rock and the occult symbolism of late seventies and eighties heavy metal. He was the originator of rock theater, leaping out of his stage coffin amid clouds of smoke. His props included a human skull on a stick, rubber rattlesnake, black bat-wing cape, and lamé turban. His parody of voodoo spiritualism was perhaps more surreal than simply comic; it took white inheritors some decades to bleach it through heavy metal ritual.

ELVIS PRESLEY

When most Americans remember the 1950s, the image of Elvis Presley inevitably comes to mind. His persona dominated the entertainment industry to become the role model of the autonomous musician, the superstar of the rags-to-riches unlimited success parable, and the renegade who symbolized rock 'n' roll's freedom from conventions of good taste. He didn't just become a hero. Elvis was the king of youth culture.

His public image definitively redefined the male performer. Men onstage were now sex objects, then and forever distinct from Hollywood heartthrobs, who bathed in more refined sentimental fantasy. The meaning of this was political as well as psychological. Male performers as real people with individual needs became secondary to the images they created. Moreover, Elvis was a man attractive to other men, who attempted for decades to become his *Döppleganger*. Few men have attempted to become Frank Sinatra or Clark Gable; many rock 'n'

rollers have tried to clone every nuance of Elvis Presley onstage. As for females, they quite often tried literally to possess Presley's body—and he narrowly escaped harm several times.

Beginning as the "hillbilly cat" or "white Negro," Presley moved to white working-class hero in the sixties, and finally, in the next decade, transformed himself into a bejeweled monarch. Never in recent history has any performer attained popularity of such mythic proportions, nor has any other rock image been published with such frequency. It is a cultural icon. In 1977, the year of his death, Presley's picture was second in volume of commercial reproduction only to images of Mickey Mouse.

It was a self-created image, not something he was born with. In Albert Goldman's *Elvis*, country singer Bob Luman recalls the nineteen-year-old Presley's costume and performance when he worked a Kilgore, Texas, stage:

This cat came out in red pants and a green coat and pink shirt and socks, and he had this sneer on his face and he stood behind the mike for five minutes, I'll bet, before he made a move. Then he hit his guitar a lick, and he broke two strings. . . . So there he was, these two strings dangling, and he hadn't done a thing yet, and these high school girls were screaming and fainting and running up to the stage, and then he started to move his hips real slow like he had a thing for his guitar.

Presley's greaser ducktail haircut, adopted in high school and slicked up with Royal Crown pomade that made his blond hair seem darker, came after he saw the 1949 film *City Across the River*, with

Elvis Presley, 1956

Tony Curtis playing the young tough, and Marlon Brando's *The Wild One* of 1953. His sideburns were an attempt to look like a truck driver. Acutely observant of Hollywood idols, Presley once pointed out to an acquaintance that Humphrey Bogart, James Dean, and Marlon Brando "never smile."

His black man's pimp outfits, from Lansky Brothers on Beale Street, Memphis, included pegged pants pleated at the high-rise waist, ballooning at the knees, with a lime-green or yellow length of side-seam cording. They were paired with a skinny suede belt, which fed through the dropped pants loops so that the buckle sat above his left hip. A loud gabardine shirt topped with a rolled "Mr. B" (for Billy Eckstein) turned-up collar completed the ensemble. Mascara appeared in 1954 at age nineteen in a Nashville recording session. The May 13, 1955, Gator Bowl performance in Jacksonville, Florida, introduced his pink suit with a lacy see-through feminine-styled shirt. David Houston, an early friend of Presley's who traveled with him during this period, reported in Goldman's *Elvis* that, "He would take the cardboard cylinder out of a roll of toilet paper and put a string in the end of it. Then, he'd tie that string around his waist. The other end, with the cardboard roller, would hang down inside his drawers so that when he got onstage and reared back with that guitar in his hand, it would look to the girls up front like he had one helluva thing there inside his pants."

Presley learned from stage experience that when he dropped to his knees in gospel crying style, his pants split. So he wore oversized outfits (which are now chic) to permit more action. In 1955 he tried out a gleaming double-breasted raw silk suit and red tie with his still dirty-blond long hair cascading onto his face. The next year witnessed bright green and red sport jackets, blue slacks, red socks, and white bucks with blue soles, darkly greased hair, and mascara-outlined eyes. It wasn't until after Presley left the army in 1959 that jet-black-dyed tresses became his trademark.

Granted, a great part of this rebel rock image was catalyzed by the 1955 film *Blackboard Jungle*, which used Bill Haley's 1954 hit "Rock Around the Clock" as an anthem—thus linking rock music to teen rebellion forever. But Presley became the visual symbol of the music and made it legend.

THE LEGEND OF ELVIS AS A REBEL PRODIGY

The contrast between Presley's stage style and life-style pointed up the carefully constructed aspect of his public performance image. Although while he was in high school Elvis wore wild clothes, his shirt collar turned up and his hair long, classmates reported that he was shy and easily intimidated. A lad whose ambition was to become a professional gospel singer, and who professed love of mom, the church, and country, he slowly reshaped his persona.

Yet the classical myth of the born hero gained ascendance over the banality of historical fact to create the legend of a child prodigy with the character of an outlaw. It took Presley five years to move from country bumpkin to macho sex symbol. His musical prowess was similarly built through trial and error while he recorded for Sam Phillips on the Sun label. He and Phillips worked out phrasing, voice quality, and final selection of material through dozens of retakes. It only seemed that the tough-looking punk, posing, gyrating, and well-hung, appeared overnight. Elvis emerged the instant prototype.

His costume was a caricature of what the middle class deemed backwoods trash, and he gave the image threatening power and a form that was repeated for decades. White teens pounced on his combination of black and country modes of music,

Elvis Presley in a publicity shot for the movie Jailhouse Rock, *1957*

Elvis Presley in a Nudie gold lamé suit, 1957

dance, speech, and clothing to consolidate a rock-abilly style that established a mythic image of a musical community. Because rockabilly was both sexy and white, it confirmed that Caucasian males were as virile as the black men who had been tearing up the rhythm-and-blues stages for the previous three decades and who were now flooding the air-waves with hot music.

Presley's glamour phase, which continued until the end of his life, began after his release from the army, when his manager decided to peddle Elvis both to Hollywood and to the night-club circuit. For

example, during a 1965 pan-Pacific performance in Los Angeles he sported a gold tuxedo jacket trimmed with rhinestone lapels, a black George Raft gangster shirt, and gold four-in-hand tie. He wore black trousers, having destroyed his matching gold lamé pair in an earlier leap from a Seattle stage.

After years of fatuous and vacuous films, Elvis needed a violent new image for a 1968 televi-sion special. Costume designer Bill Belew created a distinctive black leather suit, not in the sloppy biker style of Brando or Gene Vincent, but in the current hip mode of rising rock star/rock poet Jim

Morrison of the Doors. Bared of any metal glitter or studs, the jacket, with stand-up collar, heavy welts, paired with a broad, double-buckled strap on the wrist, and black leather pants featuring a waist-to-ankle inset leather welt on the crease that led the eyes to the famous pelvis. No ornaments or jewels of any kind—for which Elvis later became famous—marred the machismo. From that show on, Belew became Presley's designer.

The following year, in July, Presley had Belew translate his killer style into a series of karate uniforms for his engagement at the International Hotel in Las Vegas. One design was in black mohair; several were cut in the traditional two-pieces of shirt and pants, and others were jumpsuits that permitted violent gesture without midriff exposure. His macramé belt, made by a Hawaiian-Japanese practitioner of the martial arts, included congruent karate symbols. Elvis also changed his performance motions to fit the costume image: throwing karate blows, kicks, and chops, and stalking the stage like a martial artist, without so much as a pelvic thrust.

In 1970, when he returned to the same stage, he plunged into full-scale glam and beefcake with jewels and slashed décolletage on highly fitted white jumpsuits. He still possessed the svelte figure to pull it off; pearls girdled his trim waist in a karate belt of gold, while massive shining gems shot out fluorescent mauves and pinks from his fingers. Sewn-on pearls adorned his torso, and strands of them caressed his neck. He showed all off to advantage by striking a classical pose at the conclusion of each number. From then out to the end of Presley's career, Belew reveled in decorated totemic images and abstract patterns superimposed on the white expanse of jumpsuit fabric: black-and-orange-striped tigers, peacocks, Mayan calendar, Aztec pyramid, and rainbows.

Finally came the fantasy cartoon combinations of the Superman–Buck Rogers suit, high Napoleonic collars, golden Roman gladiator belt (reputed to have cost ten thousand dollars), and a lot of jewelry and scarves to be thrown to the audience. Presley's wife Priscilla initiated a cape phase in 1971 when she gave him one as a present. By January 1972, flowing, full-length, brocaded, decorated, bejeweled versions began to appear, making him into a Marvel Comics character. In his January 1973 benefit concert for the Kui Lee Cancer fund at the Honolulu International Center, televised by satellite to NBC on the mainland and also to Japan, he included the crier strip with the cape. As he finished his concluding number, "I Can't Help Falling in Love with You," he posed with legs widely outstretched, head bowed, one fist thrown outward, while an aide draped his jeweled cape onto his shoulders. After remaining in this position for a suitably prolonged interval, Presley flung the cape into the audience, gave the Hawaiian thumbs-up martial-arts victory gesture, and strode from the stage.

Elvis frequently worked the stage from one side to the other, followed by an unobtrusive attendant who looped new scarves about the King's neck as the star casually snatched them off while singing and tossed them to the fans. Costume jewelry was also flung in the same manner. His patent-leather boots, either in white, black, or blue, encased half-inch interior lifts and had inch-and-a-half heels to increase his five-foot-eleven stature to the image of one over six feet.

Elvis ended his performance career in the style to which he aspired as a teenager when he wanted to become a professional gospel singer. He almost always wore knee protectors to drop down in the full traditional gospel kneeling position when the moment called for it. His costumes approached those appropriate to black flash acts in the "Gospel Train" show at Harlem's Apollo Theatre: spectacular glitz sparkling with reflective surfaces and raw spectacle. The decorative images embroidered on his outfits were filled with loosely mythic symbolism from pagan religion—animals and hieroglyphs. He had recast black religious images and singing into white secular romance.

Each of Presley's performance and costume phases became a pattern for later rockers: his pleated pimp of the 1950s figures in the Public Image Limited's 1980s punk; his working-class greaser is reincarnated in Bruce Springsteen; his bejeweled monarch in Ozzy Osbourne's sequined robes by designer Fleur Thiemeyer. Presley's costume prototypes endure. What saved the King from ridicule was not merely his later sense of humor, which gave the whole spectacle a quality of comedy, but also that he achieved a patently artificial image, one that in no way pretended to be naturalistic. His was a mythic persona, and it passed beyond the limits of ordinary, rational human behavior.

THE REST OF THE PACK

Other hard-rocking originators either died too early to make bigger marks, lacked the creative ability to construct larger-than-life figures, or were simply self-destructive in their careers and personal lives. Gene Vincent was one of the first generation of grease-and-leather bad boys, whose first hits in 1956, "Be-Bop-A-Lula" and "Lotta Lovin," established him as an answer to Presley. Vincent did well performing in Britain in an all-black leather stage outfit, but was seriously injured in a 1960 car accident that also killed another popular rockabilly artist, Eddie Cochran. He drank himself out of his career and died in 1971.

Jerry Lee Lewis, a wilder bad boy, who was frenetic onstage, played such a perverse role offstage that he was blacklisted, barred from performing, and radio stations refused to play his records. Moreover, whereas Presley's performances were always immaculately rehearsed, Lewis was spontaneous, unpredictable, and he appeared on the verge of losing control. Yet the tension Lewis created was in itself effective in that audiences waited for him to douse his piano with lighter fluid and set it ablaze—as he had done during a concert with Chuck Berry emceed by Alan Freed. He established the American precedent for the platinum-blond rocker—and for the wearing of artificial fur trimmings. In February 1958 he appeared on the "Dick Clark Show," wearing a black tuxedo with bright artificial leopard-skin lapels and piping. In his 1958 London appearance at the Regal Cinema, his schlocking-pink suit with sequined lapels and black-ribbon tie added a touch of glitter to his ultra-wildman persona. When his career collapsed after marriage to his thirteen-year-old cousin, he returned in the 1960s to his roots in honky-tonk-style country music, but he wore dark

Jerry Lee Lewis, 1968

Chuck Berry, 1971

vested, pin-striped suits, regimental-stripe ties, and white sneakers. Although parts of his rock 'n' roll dress have resurfaced in punk and new wave artificial animal trim and long platinum hairstyles, his rocker image became too closely associated with inviolable incest taboos for anyone to adopt it wholeheartedly. Like Pan, the nature god whose name

bequeathed to us the expression "panic," Lewis appeared to possess attributes of the devil rather than those of the rebel hero. His look was associated with pedophilia and inbred southern weirdness instead of with the erotic grace of an Elvis Presley.

Chuck Berry, whose early career was also damaged by off-stage problems, was perhaps second

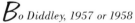
Bo Diddley, 1957 or 1958

The Duchess, 1959 or 1960

only to Elvis as the most influential artist in the rock 'n' roll sound, if not in costume. However, one of his most memorable stage outfits was an oversized white tuxedo with black lapels. While common to the big bands, formal wear was something of an anomaly for rock dance music, where the performer jumped all over the stage. Berry's outfit was so drastically en-larged to accommodate such action that he was dwarfed by it. Eighties rocker David Byrne pays homage to Berry's exaggerated costume size with his own enormous white suit. Later, Berry also performed in more sportswear and country-and-western clothes, but these ensembles never achieved the iconic quality of that huge white tuxedo.

*P*at Boone with bucks, 1957

Female rock 'n' rollers were hardly visible in the mid 1950s, though women had earlier performed prominently on rhythm-and-blues stages, in recordings, and in country-and-western music. Patti Page's cross-over country hit, "The Tennessee Waltz," became one of the best-selling records of the decade, proving that women could be musical stars. White women, like Page and Teresa Brewer, often wore modest good-girl formal wear, with bouffant skirts reminiscent of prom dresses. Black women, like La Verne Baker and the Duchess (who performed with Bo Diddley), wore the tight bad-girl second skin familiar from the established blues tradition in which club vocalists wore spangled floor-length sheaths, hobbling their feet and emphasizing their curvaceous silhouettes. The Duchess played across from Mr. Diddley, who was clad in a plaid sport coat; she wore skin-tight lamé toreador pants and high stiletto heels. It remained only for someone to invent Spandex to improve the mobility of the shiny, skinny pants look with high heels, which is now the trademark of most *male* heavy metalists. Although there was nothing intrinsically *bad* in the behavior, stage movements, or lyrics of the black bad girls, their brand of sexy look has been generally verboten to the white middle class, who perceives it as wanton, tarty, and trashy.

THE GOOD GUYS

Pat Eugene Boone, so clean that he was hardly credible, was second only to Presley in terms of record sales between 1955 and 1959. His white sport coat and white bucks became for future generations the emblem of the "good" teen idol. His copies (called "covers" in the music business) of Little Richard's "Tutti Frutti," and "Long Tall Sally" and of Fats Domino's "Ain't That a Shame" successfully bleached black rock white for millions of adolescent girls who wanted a middle-class dream idol. His appearance and stage style were in the crooner tradition, yet he still touched the rock attitude by substituting the make-believe teen world of romance for the hard earth of rhythm and blues. Although no teenager himself, he was accepted as one of them in an escapist fantasy of the eternal high school dance.

The British opted for greater realism in their counterparts of the teen idol in the late fifties. Actual young boys were costumed and coached by professionals. Cupids such as Marty Wild, Vince Eager, and Billy Fury (all protégés of manager Larry Parnes) were set up as alternatives to the adult world, whereas in America adolescents often tried to look older than their years. Except for Cliff Richard, most of the teens did not create larger-than-life images that transcended the moment. Even today, very few child idols survive to have lasting careers unless they move out of the cute phase into the creation of some persona with greater mythic resonance—as did Michael Jackson.

Buddy Holly appealed to male teens who could not project themselves into Boone's bland image and to every female taken by the combination of the slightly awkward little boy lost and a Clark Kent who could project a Superman attitude. Holly's horn-rim glasses suggested a shy intellectual while his sober suits allayed fears that rock 'n' roll was only played by idiots, maniacs, and rednecks. The allusion here was that at any moment the comic-book Man of Steel might strip off his mild-mannered cover to vanquish the powers of evil. Eighties musicians Elvis Costello and David Byrne exaggerated both the brainy—Costello used to wear Buddy Holly-like glasses and sport jackets—and unpolished stage gestures of their

Buddy Holly, 1958

prototype into more mannered representations.

THE DEATH OF ICARUS

In 1959 Buddy Holly, the Big Bopper (J. P. Richardson), and Ritchie Valens died in a plane crash, and Elvis was in exile in the army. In 1960 Eddie Cochran died, Jerry Lee Lewis was blacklisted, and Chuck Berry was in jail. It appeared that the romance was over, that Icarus had flown too high into the sun. But on another level the events also reformulated the myth of the tragic hero martyred in noble sacrifice—translated in the rock cliché as "only the good die young." That rock heroes often expire early, either by the hand of fate or their own, that they die for our rock 'n' roll salvation, has obvious messianic overtones, which are reinforced by each drug- or alcohol- or accident-related death of a star. Indeed, it has aggrandized a few who might not have occupied more than a footnote in rock history if they had been given a greater chance to display their human banalities. Perhaps the myth also inspired the next generation of rockers to take up the romance in a more tempered style closer to humble experience than the opulent and iconoclastic visions of the demised demigods of the 1950s.

Working-Class Heroes in Rock

Working-Class Heroes in Rock

Mythology traditionally supplies the symbols of initiation that carry the psyche from the images of childhood to those of adulthood. The most universally known of these symbols is the hero who appears as a guide to mark a new period or a stage in culture. This archetype takes many forms, but usually he or she is a mortal being either from fantastic tale or from historic legend who has overcome trials or limitations to achieve a quest, and who returns from it, transformed with charisma, to lead others. Diverse examples are Theseus, Psyche,

*J*ohn Oates (right) with Charlie Dechant, 1985

Promotheus, Moses, Buddha, Mohammed, and Jesus. (John Lennon's inflammatory remark that the Beatles were more popular than Jesus Christ was apt—if not statistically accurate—because the band initiated or signaled a cultural change, a mass media explosion that celebrated popular music values, which were expressed in the lyrics of their songs.) At that point, no longer belonging to the world into which he or she was born, the hero changes the culture or our perception of it. Usually the relative ease with which the hero overcomes the trials indicates that he or she is a superior being to begin with. However, it is their psychic rebirth, a recreation of their self-image, which has occurred

59

during their quest, that brings out the hero from within the previously ordinary citizen.

The rock star, while appearing to many as an overgrown Peter Pan, actually bridges the dependence of youth and the self-sufficiency of adulthood—although the rewards of being an adult are

*B*renda Lee, *early 1960s*

usually presented narrowly in performance, as revelry. Yet the "Pan" in Peter descends from the classical Greek nature deity. In addition to being known as a dangerous reveler who could incite panic, Pan invented the shepherd's pipes and bestowed bounty on farmers and fishermen who worshiped him. Only

recently has the participation of musicians in philanthropic projects introduced the idea of adulthood as a relation of responsibility to others. On the other hand, even some early lyrics of mid-fifties doo-wop songs questioned in a more-or-less adult manner the ephemeral nature of passion—for example, "Will He Love Me Tomorrow," by the Chords, or Mickey and Sylvia's "Love Is Strange." Later rock artists would dabble in politics.

The working-class rock musician who has overcome early disadvantaged circumstance to win fame and fortune often acquires legendary status and becomes an emblem of overcoming adversity. The archetype here is Prometheus.

Prometheus, a trickster hero, defied the gods on behalf of humanity. When the ancient Greek deities required man to make a sacrificial animal tribute to them, Prometheus butchered the offered oxen so that choice parts were covered with entrails, and the bones were camouflaged with fat to make them appear juicy. Zeus chose the bones. Discovering the deception, he punished the human race by depriving it of fire. But Prometheus hid firebrands in a hollow fennel stalk and smuggled them to earth. For this act of defiance he was bound in chains, and an eagle preyed upon his eternally regenerated liver. This archetype has been compared to the passion of Jesus and to the Egyptian myth of Osiris, who was slain and resurrected. In some cultures, the Promethean hero, the model for teaching arts of daring, takes on animal guises: the spider (in Melanesia), eagle hawk (Southeast Australia), coyote (North

*W*anda Jackson and Billy Tracy, *1950s*

American Indian), raven (Thlinkeet), or mantis insect (Bushman), yet is always also endowed with human qualities.

The working-class rock hero adopts the effrontery and creative spirit of Prometheus while affirming his kinship with Everyman. Separated from the bulk of humanity neither through elitist artistry nor by ruling-class birth, this figure becomes the voice for the sentiments of many. Performers of this archetype may adopt available rural, suburban, or urban outfits, so that fans can easily emulate their ensembles and cement identification with them. Others opt for more formal attire that reflects both working-class professional aspirations and dignified religious inspiration. A third group recalls the extravaganzas of the previous generation of shouter-criers—the tradition of Little Richard—and attempts to take it further.

THE COUNTRY-AND-WESTERN INFLUENCE

Although there are as many styles of country-and-western music and dress as there are in blues—from southern rural to classic, professional, and urban—there are a few constant mythic elements in country that link up with visual signs. The country music tradition generally manifests itself in a kind of anti-fashion costume. Whether it is the highly ornate, embroidered, tapered, and tailored Nudie cowboy shirt or the conservative suit and tie of the Everly Brothers, the image is one of unchanging commonality. Rock takes from country lyrics the allusions to sincerity, legendary love for open land, pioneering toughness, and a sense of unlimited freedom. Urban cowboys and coffee-house hoboes have also often fallen for a nature-boy sentimentality, which holds that those living in older, simpler environments exist in a state of grace or in greater contact with the divine.

Although there are female performers in this musical genre, the mythic origins are primarily male. Elemire Zolla's book *Archetypes* claims that the Romulus and Remus myth of the founding of Rome—itself taken from an older Near Eastern version—establishes the prototype of cowboy and pirate tales as well as stories of criminal camaraderie and exerts its strongest influence on the political imagination of Western civilization. The parable of lawless pioneer orphan brothers who marshal a male fraternity of warrior youths to create a new community justifies renegade authority. The settling of the American wilderness and the cowboy on its open range offered updated sources for recreating the archetype's romance in literature, film, and music.

In the 1930s the term *western* was added to country music to upgrade what was commonly downgraded as hillybilly hokum. Thirties popular country singer Jimmie Rodgers, who wore high-heeled cowboy boots, fringed shirts, and Stetson hat, merged the Wild West imagery of dime novels, Buffalo Bill spectacles, and cowboy-Indian-outlaw films to inspire new respect for the genre. The dumb backwoods yokel became the blazer of new trails and symbol of unfettered freedom. The Mexicanized close-fitting clothing and horse gear, plus serenading under balconies, concocted a sexy image that countered the gritty reality of the poverty and personal tragedy common to many country songs. During the two decades from 1940 to 1960, the Sad

Sack, hee-haw stereotype was successfully replaced once and for all by the film and television Westerner and, in the 1970s, by the rural outlaw hero.

Gene Autry, the singing cowboy who was most popular in the thirties and forties, did most to promote the elaborate, gaudy, brightly colored, spangled, and sequined uniforms made by Nudie of Los Angeles (outfits prized in rock music). So strong was his popular image, that, up through the fifties, most country singers, no matter where they came from, adopted the outfit.

At first, male country-influenced rockabilly, which was contemporary with Elvis Presley and Jerry Lee Lewis, followed the tradition of drape jackets and dress ties. Country-influenced performers like the Everly Brothers, Marty Robbins, and Sonny James, adopted neat suits or sport jackets. Country music still did not rate high status among the middle class.

Moreover, not until the country music resurgence of the early sixties were women singers featured as soloists in country music. Previously, they had been only members of an ensemble. One exception, Wanda Jackson, a strong contender for the title of Queen of Country Music, crossed into pop music billed as the "female Elvis Presley." She went for the prom dress instead of a female version of the male cowboy archetype and thus remained a goddess instead of descending to the realm of working-class hero. In 1959 twelve-year-old Brenda Lee sang her first hit, "Jambalaya," followed by "Sweet Nothings" and, subsequently, up to 1966, eighteen other top-twenty pop music chart hits. From a country music background influenced by rhythm-and-blues

singers Ruth Brown and La Verne Baker, Brenda Lee had a voice once described as "part whiskey, part negroid, and all woman." She even eclipsed Connie Francis as the top female vocalist in America. Like Miss Francis, who dressed down very casually in skirts and blouses during her teen-idol years, Brenda Lee represented the magically gifted child. Later, when both matured into adulthood, they wore gowns in the manner of goddesses.

Not until the country rock revival of the late sixties did the cowboy image of the 1930s and 1940s appeal to rockers in a big way. The Flying Burrito

Connie Francis, 1960

Brothers wore hippie reinterpretations of the sequined Nudie shirt embroidered with marijuana leaves instead of the traditional cactus plants and wagon wheels. The Allman Brothers, performing in country-and-western garb, preserved the unsavory redneck flavor as part of an antiurban phase. Moreover, ZZ Top continued the pageantry to an unprecedented degree in their 1976 Texas tour when, in addition to Nudie suits, they hired five tractor-trailers to haul around such western stage props as cacti, cattle, a buzzard, an American buffalo, and a thirty-five-ton, three-thousand-square-foot stage in the shape of the Lone Star state.

As for the real country singers, they were beginning to discard the cowboy look. Some wanted to look and sell like rock stars; others wanted to be outlaws; still others wanted to divorce themselves from faddish associations altogether by wearing simple sport shirts and pants. When country became fashion it no longer held the old associations of rugged individualism. Johnny Cash alternated between a black frock coat with ruffled white shirt and black skin-tight shirt and matching pants. Kris Kristofferson sang his cross-over hit, "Me and Bobby McGhee," looking like a hold-out bearded hippie from San Francisco, and Willie Nelson's Indian braids, t-shirt, jeans, and running shoes proclaimed his visual independence.

Now urban performers try to look more cowboy than the country singers do. Fringe, cowboy boots, tight western jeans, vest, Stetson, and neck scarf or string tie are apt to appear on singers who work in almost any rock style. Moreover, denim continues to return again and again in fashion, carrying mythic allusions to the American West—our equivalent of the Garden of Eden.

The musical heirs have not generally produced new costumes as much as they have worked within the existing types. Bruce Springsteen, the only American working-class hero besides Elvis Presley to achieve great mass appeal, upholds the fifties greaser tradition of leather coat, western jeans, tight, short-sleeve work and sport shirts, or t-shirts with cut-off or rolled up short sleeves. His image is ambiguous enough to be both cowhand and

*B*ruce Springsteen, 1985

*B*rian Setzer in "Teddy Boy" jacket, 1985

urban sharpshooter. His costume, like that of Elvis, evolved gradually. In 1973, when he was hailed by the press as "the new Bob Dylan," he sported a beard, wrap-around sunglasses, messy t-shirts, and generally appeared scruffy. From 1974 on he discarded the beard, sported neater, shorter haircuts, and became a clean-cut lad—even though he retained jeans, muscle-revealing tops, and sometimes even a head band. His clothes never shouted "designer," even when they were custom-ordered. He remained Everyman. Springsteen's 1983 acoustic guitar album, *Nebraska*, and fashion photography spreads by photographer Bruce Weber, such as

"Pioneers of '82," published in *Vogue*, brought western garb out of the closet again. Bands like Rank and File, Lost Lobos, Last Roundup, and Lone Justice affected the Stetsons, high-collar shirts, waistcoats, pearl buttons, scarves, and all of the other sartorial props of Hollywood that fed country and rock 'n' roll music.

Although Hall and Oates's music has been called "blue-eyed soul," their costumes have sometimes taken inspiration from country-and-western sources, Hollywood films, and the fifties greaser style. Glen Palmer, who has frequently assembled their outfits, claims that Daryl Hall often orders very specifically styled pieces such as a black western jacket with white piping. G. E. Smith, guitarist with the band, recalled that, for one of their music videos, they had Palmer recreate suits they had seen in a Humphrey Bogart film. In other performances, the band has worn the archetypal t-shirts, jeans, and leather jackets.

The Stray Cats, also clients of Glen Palmer, use contemporary reinterpretations of country-and-western themes coupled with eighties-style rockabilly-type music. Their western shirts—accessorized with contemporary jewelry—vaguely punkish bleached hair styles, and pleated pants, carry the spirit, if not the letter, of the West.

THE CHORUS

Although they took their musical skills into the streets, many popular vocal groups of the 1950s received both their training in group harmony and their formal look-alike dress style from gospel singing. Some themes of their songs paralleled concerns

The Ronettes, 1964

and group image offered a representation of ideal community, even if the song addressed only one fantasy lover.

The black fifties groups dressed *up* professionally in suits and ties in contrast to the more casual sportswear of white teen idols. The clothes were pure dandy, with men performing in sharkskin, herringbone, or camel-hair suits, with ties and white shirts. Girl groups were almost nonexistent in the fifties—except for the Chantels—since quartet singing was an all-male tradition in both gospel and barbershop genres. The vocal groups generally worked within the good-boy mode. Because black artists fought long and hard for entry into mainstream popular music, they could ill afford negative-image public relations. (By contrast, white adoles-

of the ancient chorus that accompanied Greek tragedy, which originated in religious choral odes. Like the Greek chorus, the vocal group might comment on events, speak collectively for the feelings of the audience (as in the Coasters' 1958 "Yakety Yak" or the Silhouettes' 1958 "Get a Job"), question *kismet* (Frankie Lymon and the Teenagers' 1956 "Why Do Fools Fall in Love?" or the Monotones' 1958 "Book of Love"), put forth melodrama and foreshadow events (the Angels' 1963 "My Boy Friend's Back" or the Shangri Las' 1966 "Leader of the Pack"). Romance and faith transcended personal tragedy in collective fervor, while the hymnal sound

The Shangri-Las, 1964 or 1965

cents have often idolized nasty white performers, with whom they identify and who act in ways that they cannot.) It was a white music producer, Phil Spector, who was perhaps most successful in promoting the black bad-girl look with the Ronettes.

By the sixties, record companies influenced performers' dress and their music. Motown Record Corporation was infamous for dictating their artists' personal image as well as songs. Not only did the company hire clothiers, but also charm instructors Ardenia Johnson, Maxine Powell (a professional model and actress), and Cholly Atkins to choreograph its ghetto protégés in order to enable them to entertain affluent white night-club audiences gracefully. Mary Wells, Motown's first big female star, was dressed in a tough-vulnerable combination look, with mohair and sequined sheaths, teased bouffant wig, and eyeliner-drawn, slanted, almond-shaped Egyptian eyes. Martha Reeves and the Vandellas represented the company's most adult "let's party" mode of dress, but the Supremes, the most famous of its female stars, passed through several stages of costume while retaining an ambiguous child-woman persona throughout.

In the beginning, the still-teenage girls put together their own outfits. In an interview published in Gerri Hershey's *Nowhere to Run: The Story of Soul Music*, Diana Ross described their first look-alike dresses, which they made themselves: "They were black and gold, and we had a string of gold fake pearls from the dime store. . . . You remember those balloon dresses? The skirt looked like a balloon? We made some of these in a very bright flowered print. And we had these bright orange

shoes with big flowers stuck on the front of them."

As the Supremes began to sell more records, Motown created a smoother good-girl image by dressing them in demure but figure-revealing full-length white satin sheaths with chiffon trim, white gloves, and matching satin pumps. Since the sheath dresses restricted movement, Mr. Atkins perfected a

*T*he Temptations, early 1970s

series of stylized hand motions for their performances. Finally, after Cindy Birdsong replaced Florence Ballard, more sequins and beads were applied, as the group moved into such clubs as New York's Copacabana. Their clothes and manners, drawn from the vaudeville tradition, had little to do with any attempt to woo white teens, but their glittering appeal was very successful nonetheless.

In 1968, with the release of their single "Love Child," the Supremes appeared on the "Ed Sullivan Show" in t-shirts, cut-off jeans, bare feet, and close-cropped natural hairstyles. The new look backfired because blacks felt that the Supremes

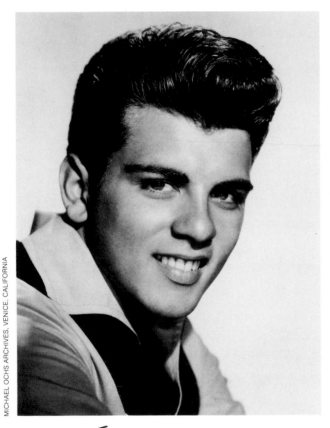

Fabian with pompadour, 1959

should present a strong positive black image, not something from the white suburbs. The group thereupon returned to glamour and became goddesses again in a television special entitled "T.C.B." ("Taking Care of Business"). They wore gowns and African-styled costumes by Bob Mackie, whose tal-

ents they used again for a follow-up special the next year, "G.I.T." ("Gettin' It Together on Broadway").

"T.C.B." also featured the Temptations, the incarnation of Motown's good-*guy* image. They were always renowned for the "sharpness of their threads" and dance steps as well as their music. Whether they wore all-white suits with embroidery on the lapels and cuffs, their bright orange, belled and sequined trouser cuffs, or sequined flames licking up their arms and trouser legs, they always impressed fans with their sense of styling. The Isley Brothers, also with Motown for a while, likewise followed the tradition of decorative stylization in their costumes.

The disposition of costumes and stylized gestures was toward elegance, or an idea of it. High stylization suggested a refinement of life toward greater professionalism and control instead of a let-it-all-hang-out amateurism. But the more refined it became the greater the distance it traveled from the mythic "vulgar" sources of its appeal. The bad-girl groups, with their skin-tight sweaters and skirts or pants, were the ones who exerted more immediate influence on the next decade's hard rockers of the rebel archetype. The Ronettes and Shangri-Las were outstanding examples, the Ronettes offering the most street-tough feminine stance, with heavily theatrical make-up and wigs piled up to the highest, stiletto-heeled shoes with fish-net stockings, and tight skirts and tops.

TELEVISION TEEN IDOLS

"American Bandstand," a nationally syndicated television show that aired from 1957 to 1969, featured teenagers dancing and guest musicians lip-synching to their recordings. More than any other single outlet, this show promoted rock culture and its fashion styles in the United States. But it was the British who were first to promote actual teen singers in the late fifties, with such adolescents as Tommy Steele (né Hicks), Cliff Richard (né Harry Webb), and Adam Faith (né Terry Nellams). There was also a weekly BBC Saturday showcase of pop music, "Juke Box Jury," in 1962 and, by 1963, an equivalent of "American Bandstand," entitled "Ready, Steady, Go." In both countries, teens self-consciously created a fashionable, cosmopolitan image of exaggerated neatness with secret signs of hipness. The side of the blouse on which American girls wore circle pins, the number and placement of vents in British sport jackets, the haircuts, the shoes all became national fashions. In addition to the professional musicians, teens also became stars and choreographed many dance fads such as The Fish, The Hully Gully, The Walk, The Jerk, The Dip, The Stomp, The Boogaloo, The Pony, and others.

The "Bandstand" audience followed the romances of the show's "regulars," wrote to them, and formed fan clubs. It was as if all the youth in the nation could become part of the Pyramus and Thisbe myth (first told by Ovid and later adapted by Shakespeare, in *Romeo and Juliet*). Pyramus and Thisbe lived next door to one another in Babylon. He, the handsomest boy, and she, the most beautiful girl in the East, they were in love but forbidden by their parents to marry. They secretly communicated with one another through a chink in the wall that separated their houses. In much the same way, mil-lions of teens rushed home everyday after school to communicate with their forbidden love objects on TV. While rock critics have tended to degrade pop vocalist idols as industry puppets paraded before stupid teenage girls, the "Bandstand" heroes attracted as many males as females to its home and studio audience. Had the show not addressed teenage mythogenic longings, it would not have prevailed so universally, or so enduringly.

The first wave of American teen vocalists were predominantly of Italian descent. "Mickey Mouse Club" Mouseketeer Annette Funicello (recording for Walt Disney Records), Frankie Avalon (né Avallone), Connie Francis (née Constance Franconero), Fabian (né Fabiano Forte Bonaparte), and Bobby Rydell (né Ridarelli), Paul Anka, and Neil Sedaka became part of the rags-to-riches rock paradigm. Although not as poverty-stricken as some earlier rockers, they had an aura of ethnic exoticism not unlike that of the Southerners' "otherness."

But such exoticism was tempered by relatively conservative dress. Sweaters, skirts, shirt-waist dresses, sport jackets or suits and ties were part of the "Bandstand" dress code. Television exposure of this kind made rock 'n' roll culture acceptable to adults, and also made the rock 'n' roll community national, the dress actually reflecting a genuine and common innocence on the part of most teens. Television teen idols, like their audiences, looked conservative and wore what they might select for school or school dances.

THE FOUR MAGICAL CHILDREN
The four young Englishmen subtly costumed as

adult-sized children embodied the mythical concept of the magical child, the brilliant prodigy, and sacred prophet, whose meteoric rise and brilliant success illuminate a generation. Examples of this character are Hercules, the infant Krishna, King David who slew Goliath, and *The Little Prince* written by Antoine de Saint-Exupery. Whereas many other teen idols attempted to dress like adults, the Beatles managed to clothe themselves in the numinous.

While many rock music groups from England became internationally famous, the Beatles were the epitome of the 1960s as Elvis was of the fifties. They were probably the most famous rock group of all time, crossing national, racial, and class barriers. They came to represent a legend, a style of values, fashion, youth, love, peace, and all the clichés as well as the good times of the mid sixties. They were the archetypal working-class hero good guys in opposition to such romantic villains as the Rolling Stones.

As the "Silver Beatles," they began in jeans and leather in imitation of Gene Vincent, and they were known for outrageous behavior on- and off-stage. After Brian Epstein became their manager, he cleaned up their image by changing their name, personnel, and clothes. They now wore Pierre Cardin-like jackets without collars or lapels, conservative American button-down shirt collars, and straight knitted silk ties. (When Ringo did not complete the knot and wore the long end of the tie *over* instead of through the knot at the neck, he provoked a minor fad.) Legend has it that their "mop-top"

*T*he Beatles, 1964

hairstyle with bangs, which made them look more childlike, was the design of the German photographer girlfriend of Stuart Sutcliff, an original member of the group who died of a brain tumor in Hamburg, Germany.

Their adult-sized little boy outfits were the antithesis of the previous English "Teddy Boy" rock style, with its heavily greased hair, large American fifties-style drape jackets, "brothel creepers"—extremely thick-crepe-soled shoes—and the "drain pipe" trousers of the working class. Neither did they copy the picturesque "Mod" (Modernist) option, the velvet Edwardian flash of the most fashion-conscious British youth, whose primary heroes were Rod Stewart and the Small Faces. The Beatles were tasteful enough to appeal to middlebrows—even in America—although there was much controversy over their longer-than-acceptable hairstyle. Until the Beatles, sexual postures of white male rock stars had been predominantly macho. The Beatles' softly flowing manes, jackets stripped of traditional male symbolism—such as exaggerated upper body proportions accented by large lapels and heavily padded shoulders—and newly acquired refinement of manners lent a slightly androgynous tinge to their image. Androgyny would be greatly emphasized by glitter rockers of the seventies.

FUNKY SOUL

As soul singer Wilson Pickett put it, "funky was something you do in the dark with *very* basic equipment." But funky music performance was also comic and religious, similar to that of pagan fertility rites, and very close to gospel.

When James Brown, the "Godfather of Soul," began performing in the late fifties, he attempted to surpass the outrages of Little Richard in order to gain notice. He processed his hair into smooth, slicked-back sides topped with a veritable mountain of wavy curls. His most extravagant glam-

*J*ames Brown, ca. 1957

our outfit was a forty-pound suit—called the "gorilla" by his wardrobe mistress—laden with studs, rhinestones, and beads. It was made by Almo Clothes, which fabricated Elvis's high-collared, studded-belt Las Vegas pieces. Brown opted for greater mobility in other outfits, such as his red jumpsuit with the slogan "SEX" stitched across the front. He discarded his shiny suits of the late fifties for cropped-to-waist-length jackets with matching vests, and tight, stretchy pants.

The humiliation of the king was a mythic part of importance in Aristotle's Dionysian tragedy, as well as in the harrowing of hell that was represented in the coronation of ancient Babylonian kings. Here a recital of the creation of the world and a last supper preceded a series of humiliations before a mock sacrificial death and final resurrection. The royal costume always included a cosmic mantle or shamanic robe. Until the mid sixties, the climax of Brown's act was usually the song "Please, Please, Please," with Brown on his knees begging and sobbing until he collapsed. Brown's aides would drape a purple cape over his shoulders, help him up, and escort him, in pain, off-stage. Brown would revive, shake off the cape, come back to center stage to launch into another chorus, again drop to his knees, and receive a gold cape. The third exercise produced a brown one, and the finale awarded him a black replica. Two other performers who were billed as rock royalty also used capes. Solomon Burke, the "King of Rock and Soul," wore them in the 1960s and 1970s, and Elvis Presley, the "King of Rock 'n' Roll," used specimens of varying length after 1971. Burke also wore an exact replica of the British Crown Jewels, a crown and scepter, for onstage coronations, complete with a cape trimmed in ermine, which dragged fifteen feet behind him. Although he played primarily to black audiences, his one crossover hit in 1961, "Just Out of Reach," made the r&b, pop, and country music charts.

*J*ames Brown, ca. 1986

*R*ick James, 1983

When Brown cut his luxurious hair in the late sixties, to accommodate the then-popular Afro look, and released his 1968 hit single, "I'm Black and I'm Proud," he punctured escapist fantasy, and had a difficult time recovering the "Godfather of Soul" success that had taken so many years to achieve. It seems that realism is as out of favor in transcendent gospel as it is in teen romance.

Although James Brown was the best-known star of the "soul" genre, others within the funk tradition also used theatrical quasi-comic dress. Wilson Pickett, "The Wicked Pickett," who became popularly known in 1966 for his "Land of a Thousand Dances" and "Mustang Sally," performed in outfits like his polkadot, shawl-collared, tightly tailored tuxedo jacket, white tux shirt with ruffled front and cuffs, and black satin bow tie.

Rick James, a 1970s heir of this tradition,

*G*eorge Clinton and Bootsie Collins, 1978

sported a funk outfit described as "Marat-Sade meets *Star Wars*": its strips of leather and vinyl accessorized with a braided and beaded hairdo, reported to have taken twelve hours to complete.

In the late seventies, George Clinton and his Parliament Funkadelics emphasized comic mode outfits designed by Larry LeGaspi, who recalls some of the costumes as follows:

There was a football helmet that I covered with fur and attached television antennas to with a fox tail hanging

off the end of each one. What was great was that you could push the antennas in and out. So when he came onstage he would pull them all the way out like a showgirl. He had one boot that came up high, and the other boot was low, with an asymmetric skirt to match the uneven boot heights. The hem had tails hanging off. This had to be in 1977.

I did a slightly shredded African costume in fake leopard skin with one shoulder hanging down. The wig I had made for him was a huge blond Afro that went clear to the floor. He walked out onstage with a spear and enormous chicken feet.

One of my favorites was a pair of elephant pants. I had actually made them for myself, but I showed them to him, and he took them. It was a pair of gray leather pants with little white elephant toenails at the feet, elephant's head with the trunk between the legs swaying back and forth, ears projecting out on the hips, and a tail in back with a little piece of fur on the end. Then I bought one of those umbrella hats on the street, and when you walked with it all on, it looked as if you were riding an elephant

Another favorite was a huge pair of bulldog shoes. They were soft sculptures I built over a pair of platform shoes. Leashes from their necks led to the wrists, so that as you walked it would look as if you were walking the dogs.

LeGaspi also created a collection of over thirty costumes for Clinton's 1978 Motor Booty tour, which was based on an underwater theme and featured octopus women, fish with huge lips in day-glo colors, sea worms, and mermaids. The "Motor Booty" girls, in padded body suits, had huge hips with plexiglass bubbles in the rear that opened up. The hot-pink worms, made of metallic fabric sewn into one long tube, were filled with bean-bag pellets and tied off with rhinestone bands into balls that decreased in size toward the tail, which was built onto a little bikini wrapped around to make a huge rear and then

extended out about ten feet back. Black angel-fish heads perched atop shoulders amid chiffon-pleated fins, surrounding the body. When the performers moved, it looked like fish swimming.

These animal costumes allude to the tradition of the bestial disguises worn by the mythic trickster of international legend. The triumph of comic costume extravagance grows from universal and timeless roots. Although, in 1968, Clinton redesigned the Parliaments from a Temptations-styled, sharkskin-clad group to the Funkadelics, steeped in psychedelic imagery, he returned to soul in 1974. As Dr. Funkenstein, in 1976, he took a preacher's role, dispensing sacraments and blessings in a crusade against those who "fake the funk." In the *Motor Booty Affair* album and tour of 1978, Clinton rapped in the guise of Mr. Wiggles—a worm and underwater disc jockey. In the eighties, he continues to perform in comic music videos, featuring a series of humorous costumes in each skit.

Although all of the costumes of the working-class hero (the cowboy, magical child, king, and comic shaman) were influenced in one way or another by television—either through inspiration via film or cartoon or by documentary live exposure—they were the last manifestations of a kind of virtuous exuberance. Before 1966, rock stars still generally took a celebratory stance toward life and love and did not strive to offend or deliberately create a counterculture. The end of innocence came with mass-media saturation coverage of confrontational politics and the popular use of recreational psychedelic drugs, which changed the outlook of the decade and the look of the rock 'n' roll star.

The Psychedelic Era

Before the bullets in Dallas, before the multiple-track electronic studio changed the sound, before the advent of LSD, there was a sweet innocence to the lyrics and look of rock 'n' roll, even when kids wore their best street-tough looks. Sexy was eyeshadow and beehives and greasy pompadour hairstyles; tight sweaters, pants, and skirts. The world was the back of a motorcycle or the seat of a T-bird.

After the Beatles wanted to hold your hand and the Beach Boys offered fun, fun, fun, Bob Dylan's early-1962 prophecy that something was blowin' in the wind heralded the explosion of rock music into mass culture, a phenomenon that seemed a multinational revolution. The times, as Dylan sang in 1964, they were a-changin'.

Janis Joplin at Woodstock, 1969

The full-scale revolt lasted from 1966 to 1970; it seemed that youth would indeed change the world, that drugs, flower power, free love, music, and mass demonstrations were overturning the evil forces of war and greed. It was a new romance in opposition to reality; and it was inevitable that bewilderment and cynicism would follow the debacle of the movement.

And that debacle was inevitable as well. In actuality, there was no mass coup d'état, but a situation aggrandized by fashion and the media, which anointed the most colorful events and entertainment extravaganzas—often one and the same—by their coverage of them. In practice, hippie politics and music were primarily expressions of the white, male middle class; they merely paid lip-service to the concerns of most of the working class, women, blacks, and other minorities. College students were

*S*trawberry Alarm Clock, ca. 1967

the primary draft resisters, while the least affluent American males traditionally joined the armed services to obtain employment training, if not a career. Heirs of middle-class parents "tuned in, turned on, and dropped out" of college and corporate careers. The self-sacrificing hippie "chick" in granny dress, sexless sack, or unisex uniform who served communal needs replaced the sexy mini-skirted child-woman of male fantasy in revolt from the autonomous suburban and urban princess.

The music and costumes reflected not life, but the imagination of life as enhanced by psychedelic drugs. The last frontier became not outer space but the human psyche, and rock music sym-

bolized all of the possibilities and hopes of the period. It became the common link that bonded youth into a culture that derived its power from opposition to the mainstream.

A popular rock group like Paul Revere and the Raiders straddled the previous era of "professional" insouciance and the genuine excesses of acid-rock dressing. Originally a hard-rock garage band founded in 1962 in Portland, Oregon, the group went to softer pop after appearing on "American Bandstand" in April 1965. With that appearance, they became overnight television staples for very young teens throughout the psychedelic years. Wearing full Revolutionary War regalia with high boots, lace shirt cuffs and frilled neckpieces, and long hair drawn back into pony tails tied with ribbons, they also became the kind of slickly packaged commodity that older college-age fans had begun to repudiate.

Professional magicians have nothing Pythian—nothing oracular, nothing spiritual—about them. They lack authenticity. They can be bought. Because his job is to control, to play upon the basest aspects of sensibility, common judgment has held that the professional magician works for evil. In this way, professional songwriter-producer-singer teams of the early sixties fell into disrepute, even though their entertainment skills were consummate. Shamans—genuine Pythians—were desired now, rock artists driven by numinous forces beyond their own control. The drug culture of the late sixties supplied these figures in abundance.

The LSD phenomenon, which spread internationally during this period, simulated for many the legendary path taken by heroes of myth. The psychedelic drug experience included all the elements of mythic legend: the initial break with ordinary reality, initiation into the spirit world of the psyche with a series of mystical encounters, and the return to daily existence accompanied by a feeling of power or enlightenment, a notion that anything and everything is possible. Acid-rock music signaled the emergence of opposition to the innocuous pre-adult world of Beatlemania, replacing it with an antiadult stance that appropriated adult privilege without the attendant middle-class values. Musi-

Grace Slick, 1974

cians singing lyrics about mystico-psycho pleasures became, for their audiences, oracles and gurus.

Acid rock, originating in San Francisco, linked up with the male-dominated mythology of the American West. On the Pacific coast, one could really see—in the flesh—Native Americans as well

MICHAEL PUTLAND/RETNA, LTD.

as Indians who had emigrated from India, and the "adult" Westerns of the sixties featured the Native American in romantic images appealing to college kids already steeped in Carlos Castaneda's peyote-based visionary tales. Consumption of LSD manufactured in the San Francisco Bay Area created a tribal community with its own legendary leaders.

The most influential of these rock prophets was the electric blues group called the Grateful Dead, the first underground band to become a hippie institution and prophet of retribalism. As the 1965 in-house band for Ken Kesey's Merry Pranksters (Johnny Appleseed distributors of LSD), they performed in whatever rumpled gear they happened to have awakened in. Known for stoned-out informality, they gave innumerable free concerts, were an integral part of the celebrated Haight-Ashbury community, and embodied the concept of musical culture as a total way of life, with the rock concert as the total experience—for which one prepared with appropriate chemical enhancers. But, unlike the later Jefferson Airplane, Big Brother and the Holding Company, and even the Rolling Stones, the Grateful Dead lacked a central charismatic leader who would become mythologized as a superstar. The folk and rural blues performance tradition from which they came featured purposefully non-theatrical, democratic community dressing. but tie-dye t-shirts, jeans, and other casual clothes never quite camouflaged their psychedelic "otherness." Despite their reputed immersion in psychedelia, poor business practices, habitual disbanding and regrouping, the band has survived into the mid eighties and continues to draw new "Dead Heads,"

as their fans are called, as well as playing to the sixties survivors. Cleaned up though they are, in Lacoste sport shirts and designer jeans, their legendary role as tribal outlaws supercedes their present attire.

Acid rock's romanticizing of the Indian—whether Native American or Oriental guru—with a touch of the Gypsy thrown in, exposed the need to identify with an "other" opposed to Establishment values and practices. The hippie rockers came to look like ersatz natives, with headbands, beads and feathers, hand-crafted embroidery, and India-made cotton clothes. The Native Americans and gurus from India, in communion with nature and with a transcendent mysticism, replaced the home-based Judeo-Christian creeds. For the white, post-Christian student, the Indian replaced the southern black as the exotic image of rock 'n' roll "otherness." This transformation had other implications, as Leslie A. Fiedler's *The Return of the Vanishing American* suggests: "In the language of the archetype, the Negro stands for alien passion and the Indian for alien perception. (Or perhaps this is only another way of saying that at the level of deep imagination the Indian is male and the Negro is female.)"

Going back even further, into ancient Greek mythology, mythologist David Miller suggested in 1970 that the then-current male type resembled Orestes, who killed his mother—emblem of security, warmth, and authority—in order to avenge the death of god the father. According to the classical myth, after Orestes destroyed his mother (Clytemnestra), whose lover (Aegisthus) had murdered his father (Agamemnon), he was pursued by the Furies (Erinyes) of his dead mother. Apollo ordered Orestes to escape the Furies by retrieving a statue of Artemis (the Roman Diana) from Tauris (the Crimea) and bringing it to Athens. There he stood formal trial, during which the Furies demanded retribution. The judges' votes were equally divided when Athena, the manly female goddess of wisdom and war, intervened by casting her vote for his acquittal and reconciled the Furies by establishing a new ritual for them. The acid rocker might be seen as Orestes suffering from the *hubris* of excessive masculinity coupled with the *erinus* of drug-influenced chthonic impulses. Like Orestes, rock culture sought salvation in Athena-like goddesses who were tough women: Janis Joplin with Big Brother and the Holding Company, and Grace Slick of the Jefferson Airplane.

THE GODDESSES OF '67

As in all romance, what belongs to and helps shape the hero is his or her opposite, a strong rival who is worthy of contest. Perhaps there can be no complete leader without provocation from others of equal but contrasting style (even within the "good" or "bad" genres themselves). As with the genres of the fifties and early sixties, the acid-rock contingent produced its polar deities.

Grace Slick and Janis Joplin were the most popular examples of the Athenian goddess in both her dark and light aspects. Grace Slick was the hip, cerebral, icy ex-fashion model beauty with a piercing soprano voice. Her avowed drugs of choice were psychedelic, "good" drugs in the view of college-

JOHN LEE/STAR FILE

Stevie Nicks, 1983

age middle-class fashion, because they were consciousness-expanding. By contrast, Janis Joplin's publicly known recreational outlets, heroin and alcohol, were objectionable to those who were into Oriental mysticism. Joplin, often overweight, sloppy, swearing, drunk, bisexual, was an overwhelming rock star rebel. In contrast to the metaphoric head-trip Slick delivered, she spilled out her emotions onstage. While the Airplane's open evocation of a new community was the call for the West's New Eden, Joplin exalted the individual. She was one of the guys, but really vulnerable underneath her rough exterior. Her outfits were the image of complete autonomy from Seventh Avenue fashion: collages of thrift-shop fur, feathers, costume jewelry of every vintage, sleazy satin draperies, and tangled hair. An orgiastic song delivery made her performance the apotheosis of raw emotion in the crier-shouter blues tradition. Although Grace Slick's outfits, with symbolic psychedelic graphics of stars, stripes, and bright colors, were neater and more theatrically conventional as costumes, she wore them with the determined conviction of an angry warrior. Both women dominated their bands visually and took the spotlight in performance style as well.

Joplin's death from a heroin overdose in 1970 sealed her mythic status as a messianic rock martyr. Slick's Jefferson Airplane disbanded, reformed under a recombination of members, and she has continued to work periodically into the 1980s. But without the context of the mythical ideal community, and without another goddess counterpart of equal intensity, another Joplin, the urgency of her stance dissipated as the acid dream ended. Both female incarnations of

*L*inda Gravenites design for Janis Joplin, 1969 — "Blouse: black silk chiffon figured in velvet/paisley design. Pants: black panné velour/elastic waist."

Athena were the first women to become superstars in the predominantly male-dominated counterculture as well as in the pantheon of rock 'n' roll.

While neither Slick nor Joplin would have identified herself as Athena, the later soft-rock post-hippie heir of the 1970s, Stevie Nicks (formerly with Fleetwood Mac), created the stage role of another goddess, Rhiannon, from Celtic mythology. Nicks even called herself a good witch. In an interview, she told the story of the mythological goddess who surrendered her kingdom in the sky in order to marry a mortal. Although forfeiting her power, Rhiannon retained the ability to predict the future. Nicks chose layers of chiffon, lace, diaphanous scarves and shawls, suede boots, silk hats, and flecks of glitter on her cheeks and hair to portray her character. She developed her fairy-tale image in the mid seventies, changing from her previous outfits of bell-bottom jeans, t-shirts, and sweaters—the "costume" of her audience. Her soft femininity contrasted with the previous hard-edged imagery of the late sixties goddesses of warfare—indeed, it signaled the end of that era.

THE GYPSY

Jimi Hendrix was the only solo male artist whose mythic stature compared with that of Janis Joplin. (Jim Morrison of the Doors, while acting the rebel hero, too often discredited himself as a shaman in favor of playing the drunken fool.)

Although Hendrix worked with James

*J*imi Hendrix at Woodstock, 1969

Brown, Little Richard, the Isley Brothers, Wilson Pickett, and Jackie Wilson, his music was so individual and his outfits so far outside those of the black musical community, that his fans were drawn from among white students who prized eccentric experimentation. His arrogant stage performances were the antithesis of the stylized black vaudeville of Motown as well as the gospel self-humiliation of

$\mathcal{S}$ergeant Pepper's Lonely Hearts Club Band *album cover, 1967*

Brown. He looked and sounded egotistical, maniacal, and weird. He took the crying-shouting mode and translated it into soaring, screeching guitar sounds that no one had ever heard before. In image and action, Jimi Hendrix was the nomadic gypsy, the swarthy "other" of romance mystery who moved from country to country, from black to white musical worlds, to become an acid-rock cultural hero. Iain Chambers, in *Urban Rhythms*, noted Hendrix's

"black–Red Indian gypsy costume" consisting of "Afro-hair, amulets, headbands of fringes, flamboyant jewelry, bandana, boots, and much Oriental finery."

He began rock costuming with a Navajo vest, high cavalry boots, and purple gaucho hat pulled down to his ears. During his sojourn in England, where he formed a trio with British musicians Mitch Mitchell and Noel Redding, he adopted paisley Edwardian jackets, shirts with embroidery and decorative piping, love-bead necklace, sash, and tailored high-waisted trousers. At his famous Monterey Pop Festival performance in 1967, where he set his guitar on fire, he wore a paisley headband, profusely and widely ruffled shirt, embellished vest with decorative frog fasteners, and tight jeans-styled pants. A star at twenty-four and dead at twenty-seven (of a drug-related accident), he joined the other mythic, sacrificial rock heroes. His performance style, music, and gypsy eclectic mode of dress has lived on, resurrected in heavy metal rock.

Despite the stardom of Jimi Hendrix, the psychedelic rock scene had little to say to blacks until Sly (né Sylvester Stewart) and the Family Stone addressed the ideal of an interracial rock community—not merely in their lyrics, but also in the look and composition of the group. Sly's mixed gender and racially integrated band dressed in psychedelic finery and also dabbled in glitter. His 1969 single hit "Everyday People" and 1970 "Everybody Is a Star" expressed musically what the variety of individual outfits reinforced visually. The gypsy maverick, Sly Stone's cross-over style would later influence the disco era.

The Rolling Stones, 1979–80 tour

THE BRITISH CONTINGENT

The British version of the picturesque psychedelic rock costume style recalled legendary uniforms of the Empire, the dandified gentility of the class system, and the high decoration of Pre-Raphaelitism and the Arts and Crafts movement. Paisley designs first entered England on a systematic basis via the East India Trading Company starting about 1600, and the tailored paisley haberdashery of some 350 years later evoked a civilized pastoral manor where people, tea roses, and romance thrived. The Beatles adopted this longing for a paradisiacal past by wearing comfortable, embellished versions of high-collared nineteenth-century ersatz military uniforms for their 1967 album cover of *Sergeant Pepper's Lonely Hearts Club Band*.

By contrast, the Rolling Stones continued to expand their popularity as the counterpoint twentieth-century villains—more through their transgressive attitude, misogynist lyrics, and off-stage drug busts than through any particular visual emblems they wore onstage during the acid years. As a group, the Stones couldn't qualify for genuine mythic stature as working-class heroes (since Mick Jagger and Brian Jones were former college students), nor did they qualify as Daedalus the artist, since they did not write as many of their own songs as the Beatles did. But with a charismatic leader—Jagger singing "Sympathy for the Devil"—they pursued the demonic route until brutality and murder at their Altamont (California) concert demonstrated where that would lead. During the seventies, the Stones's outfits became increasingly theatrical in contrast to their early street clothes. In the tradition

*J*ohn Entwhistle and Roger Daltry of the Who, 1978

of flamboyant black performers, "white Negroes" in sound and visual style, the Rolling Stones retained the necessary mythic "otherness" to carry on after the Beatles' demise.

The Cream, at the peak of their success in 1968 (just before disbanding), impressed fans not only with their musical virtuosity in interpreting rock blues, but also with their fashionable costumes: polkadotted pants, neck chains, fringed suede shirts alternating with paisley prints, and long flowing locks. They held the spotlight for a

moment, but they lacked the lasting cohesion necessary to be Pythian shamans or to represent a sense of mythic community.

Although Pete Townshend protested, "We never were Mod!" the Who's outfits were nevertheless what most Americans considered to be Mod. Actually, Townshend's most flamboyant ensembles were closer to costume than to fashion. His early gold lamé jacket and frilly cuffs, and Roger Daltry's bouffant hairstyle were the antithesis of the Mod neatness, short haircuts, Fred Perry sport shirts, and smart combinations of French, Italian, and Carnaby Street fashion. When Townshend was the first to wear the Union Jack onstage in England, it was far more inflammatory than American hippies donning the Stars and Stripes in a place where patriotism was out of style during the Vietnam years. Townshend also sported an outfit graphically decorated with pound (instead of dollar) signs. Differing from other groups, who tended to fix a set of stylistic options, the Who did not adopt a uniform look for any length of time, and each member of the band preserved his individuality. This did little to enhance the group's stature as proponents of the tribal community, but it did make it more possible for individuals to cultivate solo careers later. While they often lapsed into popular dress, their most rebellious outfits provided more punch than chic.

British odd-ball Arthur Brown, an ex-philosophy student and originator of the theater of shock rock, performed in 1967 with striking make-up and costumes, including a metal helmet that he

*R*oger Daltry of the Who, 1978

MICK ROCK/STAR FILE

MICKEY ADAIR/STAR FILE

Iggy Pop with dog collar and lamé gloves, 1970

would set ablaze at the end of his act. He wore phosphorescent robes (alternating with asymmetrically different pants and jackets), black-and-white face paint, and a series of metal masks to perform his spastic version of dance and song, his voice metamorphosing from gentle softness to screeches within seconds. The British billed him as "God of hell fire" in mid 1968, but his private mythology was out of synch with English taste and times. Not until the seventies did Alice Cooper develop the horror style again. Then it became part of mass culture, whereas Arthur Brown's act had remained mere novelty.

PSYCHEDELIC ART MOCK

After the Beatles joined the acid heads, it seemed like the whole culture was approving psychedelic fashion. Moreover, by the late 1960s, their music was being discussed seriously as art. The associated costume style became not only respectable but also middle class and even sacrosanct. Acceptance of pop culture by the academic establishment made wearing rock-associated accoutrements part of mainstream dressing. Even some businessmen sported Nehru-collar leisure suits, long hair, beards, and beads. It was time for the zany harlequins to emerge.

In January of 1968 Frank Zappa and the Mothers of Invention parodied the cover image of the *Sergeant Pepper* album with their own album entitled *We're Only in It for the Money*. Instead of trying to look pretty, as did most Beatles imitators, they were purposefully ugly—in gestures, noises, appearance, and even song titles: "You're a Beast," "What's the Ugliest Part of Your Body," "Nasal Retentive Calliope Music," "Let's Make the Water Turn Black," and "Hot Poop." Actually, like the traditional wise fool, Zappa the joker seemed the only sane person around, the antidote to mock a world gone mad. Decorative shirts and pants were fun, drugs were recreational escapes, but when fashion associated itself with high art and religion, the trickster intervened.

Depending on whose viewpoint one entertains, Iggy Pop (né James Jewel Osterburg) and the Stooges were either "the spirit of W. C. Fields, The Three Stooges, The Marx Brothers, and Elvis Presley" combined, or the dark violent precursors of Alice Cooper, or the angry prophets of punk. Their first album of 1969, *The Stooges*, was described as "track after track of three-chord slobbering rock 'n' roll," which mocked virtuoso rock musicians—professional magicians as opposed to inspired shamans—as well as the middle-class gentrification of rock. Iggy reportedly vomited onstage, was beaten, rolled on lit cigarettes, and was photographed nude (except for a bow tie and dollar bill pasted in a strategic spot). He was prone to going bare-chested, the better to smear his upper torso with peanut butter or rake it with shards of glass. The 1969 through 1973 albums were rereleased in 1977 because of their popularity with British punk and new wave fans, and Iggy Pop made five solo albums (one, *The Idiot*, was produced by David Bowie). No matter how one interprets their act, the Stooges were legendary originals from whom later rockers chewed off many bits and pieces. During the early eighties, Iggy Pop collaborated with David Bowie as a songwriter, and in late 1986 Iggy released a new solo album with a tidy cover image of himself as a serious, hard-working rock artist—in jeans and t-shirt—which replaced his early unsavory, demented persona.

Perhaps polite society's takeover of psychedelic costume contributed to the demise of the counterculture as much as any political disillusionment did. How could one look like an outlaw in opposition to the Establishment when the Establishment was wearing their clothes? The next hard rock groups had to up the shock ante in order to create a look that wouldn't be as eagerly and blissfully consumed by adults.

Glitter and Glam Rock

To speak of authenticity in the same breath as glitter rock may seem preposterous, but the seventies redefined the criteria of validity in rock 'n' roll just as each previous decade had. A bona fide rock or folk singer in the fifties had to be poor, Southern, or black (preferably all three). In the sixties, one didn't actually have to be one of the "folk," but identifying with the sentiments of your song was essential, and you had to "do your own thing." In the seventies, the success of the Beatles as "artists" (after their 1967 *Sergeant Pepper* album) made it not only credible but also admirable to create concept albums and also fictional characters. Moreover, it was no longer possible to walk out onstage and simply be oneself—not in the giant

David Bowie as Ziggy Stardust with the Spiders from Mars, ca. 1972

arenas that were increasingly serving as rock's venues. To be natural was to fade into the surroundings. To make oneself seen at great distances, theatrical dressing was a necessity.

Even before the sixties had ended, the idea of the rock concert as theater had become absorbed into the mainstream. Broadway featured the rock musical *Hair* in 1967, then *Jesus Christ Superstar* in 1971, and the Who performed *Tommy*, written in 1969, at the Metropolitan Opera House, Lincoln Center, in New York City. Moreover, both in Europe and America, avant-garde theater productions had been for decades breaking all the rules of psychological realism. In hard rock there was a trend on the part of new bands to dissociate themselves from the hippie jeans and t-shirt look and nostalgic soft country sound. Thus, the already established use of highly stylized costumes from earlier black rock heroes made the move to dramatic rock dressing almost inevitable. Throughout the mid seventies, Bob Mackie's designs for Cher's television shows conditioned middle America to expect glamour from rock 'n' rollers.

Glitter, or "glam," rock gave rise to a glamorous style of rock dressing often, but not always, associated with androgyny. Although this style was present in each decade of rock to varying degrees, it reached a peak between the end of the 1960s and 1975. It was associated with no single style of music, but generally fell within two polar traditions: popular vaudeville and avant-garde theater. Glitter rock was both visual art and rock gone pop. It also represented a kind of politicized thinking, a theatrical idea about singing different from the traditional psychological one, for it separated the stage persona from the personality of the performer. To be theatrical is to play outside the event or character observed. In the avant-garde theater of the early seventies, it meant dropping the "fourth wall," traditional theater's illusionistic "glass" barrier between actor and audience. The performer took on the fictional role at the same time as he or she dropped the "fourth wall" and courted the real-life audience. In rock, any stage role was valid if the person performed with intensity; one could wear glitter and not necessarily be a transvestite yet still be authentic. One could also, like Bette Midler, mock the role onstage, so that comedy might distance the fans and separate the performer from the role she played in order to create an aesthetic space between the two.

At its most sophisticated, glitter rock approached theatrical art. At its worst, it became campy farce. In practice, fans generally sought to read autobiography into fictional images and lyrics. Of course, what made glitter rock so international was that its images could be enjoyed on different levels—from the idea of rebellion against social and sexual repression, to sheer visual entertainment and spectacle, to mythogenic appeals to the unconscious. Of all these, the mythological element was perhaps the most widespread.

GLITTER AND ANDROGYNY IN MYTH

Glitter is nothing new either in entertainment or religion. When the court of Christian Byzantium from the fifth to the thirteenth century A.D. featured glittering lions of gold that wagged their tails and roared, birds of metal and gems singing in jeweled trees, the Byzantine bishops and kings adopted spangled ceremonial vestments the further to carry off the spectacle of man-made paradise and to make followers mindful of the luminous other world. History also records that beholders of visionary experiences often see objects encrusted with gems and that landscapes and figures appear with spectacular luminosity. Plato stated that the other world shines and glows with a kind of fire; the biblical book of Ezekiel records a vision of paradise with precious stones; and Revelations speaks of a heavenly city of jewels. Medieval and Renaissance clerical vestments, which are so finely recorded in Northern European altarpieces and donor portraits, incorporated reflective satins, silks, jewels, and precious metals, which separated the holy clergy from the profane followers.

Performers in circuses, minstrelsy, and vaudeville, right up to Hollywood films and Broadway musicals, continued to fulfill the desire to transcend the ordinary and enter a supernatural world of romance. The rock 'n' roll singer was certainly not the first to use glittering costumes, but he made mass acceptance of the androgyne a valid masculine posture that differed from the campy female impersonation that had caricatured women. While Little Richard was the first popular rock star to popularize both glittering costumes and androgyny for a white teen audience, he was considered in his time an aberration. Later pop and soft rockers linked up with white vaudeville, and harder rockers took a radical theatrical position of confronting conventional sexual roles. There was safety in numbers, so it wasn't daring in the seventies for heterosexual men to wear costumes with feminine associations.

The androgyne and hermaphrodite were the original mythic expressions of wholeness, which symbolized perfection in pagan, Gnostic, and Oriental beliefs. Mythologist Mircea Eliade stated that the primordial divinity itself was both male and female, and the earliest description of Adam in an ancient Hebrew text proclaimed that he was "man on the right side and woman on the left, but God has cloven him into two halves." Traces of androgyny occur in such vegetative and fertility deities as Attis, Dionysus, Cybele, and the Aztec Coatlicue, who assumed combined male and female forms under the name of Centeotle. Androgyny became an attribute of autonomy, strength, and wholeness—in short, of an ultimate being. In Gnostic Christianity the Fall was seen as the result of the separation into

two sexes, and the return to paradise was seen as a return to the original androgynous state of the angels achieved through discipline and the ritual of the *sponsa Christi,* the bride of Christ, in which men and women lived together like angels, who are both sexless and immortal. This was like the Hindu

*T*he Commodores, 1978

brahmacharya, which Gandhi practiced in his later years, sleeping with young women in his entourage to confirm his commitment to celibacy. But Gnosticism was also a male religious system, in which the theme of fear of sexual power figured strongly along with the need for women to fit into programs of male purification.

Hermaphrodite, the off-spring of Hermes (known to the Romans as Mercury) and Aphrodite (the Roman Venus and, earlier, the Babylonian Ishtar and Phonecian Astarte), Eros (the Roman Cupid), and the Oriental Bodhisattva, in their bisexual forms, were all symbolic of a perfect state of being in which duality is abolished. (The Yin-Yang symbol of time is itself represented as the union of the dark, feminine earth and the light, masculine sun as a complete union, which makes manifest *Tao*, The Way, cosmic order, truth, and right conduct.) According to Robert Graves's *Greek Myths*, the concept of the androgyne, which evolved in Greece in pre-Hellenic times during the transition there from matriarchy to patriarchy, was ritually institutionalized when sacred kings, deputized as Hermaphrodite to rule for the Great Goddess, were adorned with artificial breasts. This shift was explained by an Orphic cosmic creation story still told in Homeric times. The tale stated that, at night, the Goddess, courted by the wind, laid a silver egg. Eros, who hatched from this egg, was double-sexed and golden-winged. Now, myth declared that *he* created the earth, sun, and moon, but that the Great Goddess ruled the universe until she passed her scepter to Uranus. (Marilyn French's *Beyond Power* estimates that the advent of patriarchy took place around the third millenium B.C.)

Plato's *Symposium* explains sexual attraction through the character of Aristophanes, who recounts that, in the beginning, the race was divided into three types of beings created by the Cretan mother goddess Rhea. Besides females and males, there was a third being with doubles of all parts. These hermaphrodites, who were superior to other humans in strength and energy, attempted to oust the gods from heaven. In retaliation, Zeus sliced each double in half to reduce its power, whereupon each bisected being flung itself into the arms of its original half and clung to it. Seeing that these now immobilized pairs would die of starvation and that nothing would ever be accomplished, Zeus separated the individual halves, scattering them abroad. But the lovers continued to seek their other half, hoping to be made whole again.

According to Robert Graves's *The White Goddess*, pagan Europe had no male gods at the start of the Neolithic Era, and later symbolic consorts of the goddess here on earth were ritually sacrificed to assure agricultural rebirth. Laming and emasculation became less drastic substitutes for murder; later still, circumcision; finally, in the Hittite kingdoms, the wearing of buskins (also called *cothurnus*) became the rite. In the pre-buskin era, the sacred king was ritually lamed in such a way that he had to wear high-heeled shoes in order to walk. Mercury's winged sandals, also those of Theseus, Perseus, and Hermes come from this tradition. Hermes was generally represented as standing on tiptoe, because the holy heel was raised.

GLITTER AND THE VAUDEVILLE TRADITION

Vaudeville began in America as an alternative to the beer hall, which specialized in comic skits with risqué dialogue, smutty musical routines, and situation plots. Family-oriented variety halls now featured a broader range of acts with song, dance, comic skits, acrobats, and drama. Although glittering costumes and flashy properties were a permanent part of the circus, they entered the American variety stage in the 1870s, when entrepreneur J. H. Haverly transformed the minstrel show into a dazzling extravaganza that included huge numbers of performers in magnificent costumes. According to Douglas Gilbert's *American Vaudeville*, the first "clean" vaudeville in America, one that played to a "double audience" of men and women, opened in New York's Tammany Hall in 1881. The genre began to aim for "refinement" in the 1880s with lavishly costumed production numbers performed without blackface. One American company even dressed the cast in Shakespearean costumes.

Vaudeville thrived until the 1920s, when film replaced it as popular entertainment. Although some Broadway musicals and nightclub acts in Las Vegas and similar resorts continue the live performance tradition, it was Hollywood film-costume design, from the celluloid musical heirs of the 1930s through the 1950s, that influenced popular music costume and then rock 'n' roll. From John Harkrider's film outfits through Bob Mackie and Fleur Thiemeyer, an unbroken tradition of glamorous *chanteuse* glitter still thrives. Continuing the vaudeville legacy are the rock 'n' roll road shows for which thousands are spent on costumes and millions on presentation of the staged productions (as well as music videos).

In the 1970s, rock 'n' rollers restored some of the original raunchiness and vulgarity of the nineteenth-century barroom minstrels through onstage simulation of sexual acts (with their guitars) and deliberately provocative costuming, which blurred gender identification. However, along with the bad boys of hard rock, a lighter, cleaner, more youthful pop singer type emerged to bridge the gap between middle and low culture, with a glittering image deriving from later vaudeville. Less abrasive to popular taste than the sound and imagery of adult males in drag was the teen androgyne who was still part child and especially attractive to younger adolescents. In 1966–67, young British model Marc Bolan (né Feld) belonged to the first-ever glam rock band, John's Children, before he formed Tyrannosaurus Rex in 1968. Originally working within an underground or anticommercial folk-based music, he became a teen hero in glitter and satin, singing very commercial pop songs written by professional songwriters. Bolan claimed that performers like Fred Astaire and Mae West were his inspiration for the glamour image. Following in his footsteps were David Cassidy, the Bay City Rollers, Garry Glitter (né Paul Raven), and the Sweet. Alvin Stardust (né Bernard Jewry but calling himself Shane Fenton in the early sixties) was the most improbable of teeny glitterati. A fat middle-aged clown who in 1970 sported Gene Vincent-style black ensembles with long gloves, Stardust moved into silver-sequined jumpsuits to sing such tunes as "My Co Co Ca Choo" and "You, You, You" in 1973. The Sweet also started with innocuous pop bubblegum like "Co-Co" (1971), "Wig Wam Bam" (1972), and "Funny, Funny" (1971), but their androgynous costumes gradually became more bizarre and lyrics turned to such screamers as "Teenage Rampage," "Hell Raiser," and "Ballroom Blitz" in 1973.

While the teen idols worked within the pleasing "music hall" tradition of glitter, the New

*M*arc Bolan, 1974

*G*ary Glitter, ca. 1973

York Dolls burlesqued their material within the rude barroom mode. The Dolls reached their peak of popularity in the New York City art scene at The Kitchen, a showcase for avant-garde performance in 1972 and 1973. Although never more than cult figures in their day, the Dolls influenced the later glitter costumes. They probably gained more notoriety from their drag queen wardrobes than from their music, which was reputedly Rolling Stones circa 1964. Satin tops with bare midriffs, flowered dresses, stockings with lots of runs, three-inch spike heels got lots of press mileage. *Variety Magazine* called it all "way-out gimmicry for eye and ear, and as rockers go, total entertainment," while *The Village Voice* labeled them as four "mincing prancing males who look like they've been whisked off of a Bushwick corner, run through Kenneth's salon in the dark, outfitted at the Volunteers of America,

The New York Dolls, 1973

given a shot of B-12 and crystal meth, and sent howling on the stage." Although camp was nothing new, dragging it out of the closet into popular rock culture under the camouflage of "entertainment-as-resistance-to-bourgeois-culture" enlarged its following within a heterosexual audience.

Perhaps the most successful contemporary glitter star has been Michael Jackson. His ability to alter his stage image with the times has allowed him

to escape the narrow confines of the magic child archetype to that of the double-sexed, golden-winged Cupid. Although his glittering sequin and satin costumes are indeed eye-catching, what is most unusual about his appearance is his recreated face. In contrast to Hollywood aspirants who do their makeovers before they get on film, Jackson made his plastic surgery transformation after he was already an established pop singer. The metamorphosis of his

formerly virile male black visage into one suggesting a white female model, plus the relaxation of his formerly kinky locks into looser curls, turned him into a striking androgyne with multiracial appeal. Both Jackson's facial make-over, which has caused him to resemble a female impersonator, as well as his increasingly lavish glittering dress locate the historic origins of his costume within the white vaudeville tradition. The late white minstrel show aspired to a level of refinement approaching theater art, unlike burlesque, which offered comedy centering on the apertures of the human body. White minstrel acts in the 1850s and 1860s featured men clothed in female dress playing women with such dignity and delicacy that the press considered the act perfectly reputable. By 1873 the female impersonator was indispensable to a troupe, and in 1882, Francis Leon, a white minstrel female impersonator in vaudeville was not only the highest paid performer but one of the most praised of that day.

Jackson progressively refined an aristocratic pose: first with preppy casual wear, white socks and cashmere sweaters, gradually adorned with elaborate brooches and rhinestones, then finally with European-styled fantasy uniforms, which were progressively encrusted with epaulets, braids, and big shiny buttons. Designer Danny Whitten produced six pairs of the famous rhinestone-covered gloves, two in black, one pair in red white and blue, and the rest in white.

Although circuses have worked for centuries within the tradition of glittering costumes, these

The New York Dolls, 1975

tended to be vulgar and outright sexy rather than effete or androgynous. By contrast, the refinement of Jackson's costumes recalls the legacy of the white minstrel show after the 1880s. When the appearance of authentic black minstrels challenged the hegemony of whites performing in blackface, white minstrels worked up large touring companies with lavish glittering costumes and sets and left the original plantation-oriented songs to the blacks. Working one-night stands and limited-run performances, much like the contemporary rock road tour of the Jacksons, the white minstrels homogenized their material by removing raucous elements, so that the shows were as acceptable to Iowa audiences as to those in New York City. One theater exit poll showed that the average attendees of Jackson's mid-1980s Victory Tour were two middle-income white parents with two children between the ages of six and fifteen. His consummately tasteful and thoroughly professional style of performing, combined with an off-stage image of religiosity and abstemiousness, ranks him with the "good guys," despite obvious cross-gender visual references.

By contrast, wearing glam outfits that change from year to year and very obvious make-up, Prince plays the bad boy within the rhythm and blues and soul music heritage of James Brown, in which men may look like dandies—but there is no doubt about their masculinity. Moreover, the falsetto Prince frequently uses comes from male African tradition, rather than from a desire to impersonate a woman. His image is antagonistic to formal white culture, and he mocks his rock music critic admirers in his 1982 song "All the Critics Love U in

New York" by listing the absurd things he can do onstage and still be praised, summing up with "the reason you're cool is that you're from the old school." If Jackson's image is an idealized version of black bourgeois aristocracy, Prince is the urban hustler who scorns it. As the common man raised to the level of hero, he appropriates whatever accessories will challenge WASP taste and arrogantly struts his stuff in outfits that reveal more and more flesh. His 1986 film *Cherry Moon*, which he directed himself, not only showcases his songs and costumes by Marie France, but delineates his Staggerlee folk hero stance of the black rebel. From the 1980 album cover of *Dirty Mind*, with costume of bikini briefs and open jacket with highly stylized wide lapels, heavily padded shoulders with studs, accessorized by a flowered neck scarf, long black stockings, and very high-heeled boots, he moved through Edwardian paisley and ruffles, purple stripper bird's-eye lamé, a fantasy gaucho look with wide-brimmed hat, and began paring the outfits down to very short, cropped knit tops and very tight pants with high-heeled boots. As with most performers who are highly exposed in the media, he seems to have learned the necessity of continual shifts in costume while retaining a constant archetypal style.

The majority of white glitter rockers from Britain, ranging from the most enduring, such as Rod Stewart and Elton John, through the most ephemeral, like Alvin Stardust and Gary Glitter, worked within the vaudeville tradition of their

*M*ichael Jackson, 1984 Grammy Award ceremonies, and with the Jackson Five, ca. 1975. Right: Prince, 1984

native land. The performers who have lasted into the eighties have learned to update their costumes while also retaining a tinge of androgyny if not all-out glamour. Bob Mackie has designed Elton John's ensembles for his 1986 world tour, and Fleur Thie-

Sheila E., 1984 American Music Awards

meyer works with Rod Stewart. Other performers who work within the brutal heavy metal mode, moved into the eighties with glam outfits to soften the harshness of their images and even add humor to their representations. Boy George (né George O'Dowd) captured much attention with his eighties version of glam style (aided by designers Martin Degville, Sue Clowes, and Dexter Wong); young

teens, not old enough to have experienced David Bowie's costume extravagances, enthusiastically embraced the dress-bedecked Boy George as a brand-new image. Bowie had worn dresses both on- and off-stage in 1971, but photographs of these were removed from album covers in the United States.

THE ART SCHOOL CONNECTION

After the Beatles' success in the mid and late sixties, rock as a career attracted both American youths trained in the visual arts and also some who were even acquainted with literature. The rock musician was a hero comparable in critical stature to the artist, and entertainment was viewed as rebellion against convention. Fine arts schooling, classical music training, and liberal arts programs attracted primarily middle-class students, some of whom soon began to influence rock 'n' roll. Bob Dylan, a drop-out liberal arts student, and Jim Morrison of the Doors, a poet and former film student, demonstrated awareness of literary tradition in the mid sixties. In 1966 a group called the Falling Spikes (and before that the Warlocks, which was also the original name of the Grateful Dead) renamed themselves the Velvet Underground and played in pop artist Andy Warhol's multimedia environment, "The Plastic Exploding Inevitable," which featured the band, stroboscopic lights, and Warhol's films. The male members of the group—Lou Reed, John Cale, and Sterling Morrison—all had classical training. Maureen Tucker on drums did not, and neither did Nico, the singer who was visually skilled in designing and making her own costumes. Although the group worked within Warhol's aesthetic of urban trash, they were responsible for their own visual and aural elements and performed such ditties as "Heroin," "Waiting for the Man," and "I Want to Be Black." Betsey Johnson, then a recent ex-fine arts student from Pratt Institute and Syracuse University, was asked by John Cale to do their stage outfits. She recalls: "I was at Max's [Max's Kansas City] and the Chelsea [Chelsea Hotel], and I had just started designing for Paraphernalia. You couldn't separate music from art from clothing from hairstyles and makeup. . . . John wanted to wear masks; he wanted his hands on fire and gray tight suede pants. But Nico had a clear idea of what she wanted for each performance. One time she wore a beautiful St. Laurent-type white gabardine pantsuit. The next day she'd be sewing a monk's gown out of burlap bags." In short, a concept of singing performance as an ironic art replaced "sincere" messages from the heart; and costume now represented theatrical rather than psychological character.

In England, art schools of the sixties had liberalized entry requirements. They took both sixteen- and seventeen-year-old working-class teens who neither fit into trade school nor college-entry programs and also middle-class youths who were equally unsuited to conventional schools. Rock stars like John Lennon, Keith Richards, Peter Townshend, Eric Clapton, Jimmy Page, Brian Eno, and David Bowie all moved into rock 'n' roll from art school training. Of these, David Bowie (né David Jones) became the most famous for developing glitter rock into a comprehensive spectacle, encompassing lyrics, a fictional hero, and costume.

According to rock critic Tom Carson, Bowie "almost single-handedly moved rock 'n' roll into a new era—redefining rebellion as entertainment, and entertainment as subversion, changing forever his audiences' perception of the form and opening it

*Lou Reed, from the* Rock 'n' Roll Animal *tour and album cover, 1973*

up to possibilities heretofore unimaginable." Moreover, he celebrated the creative artifice of the stage persona and made rapid, successive image-shifting a precedent regularly followed by contemporary rockers. For those wanting to believe in the reality of the permanently possessed musical shaman, Bowie represented the ultimate heresy—a faker. For those

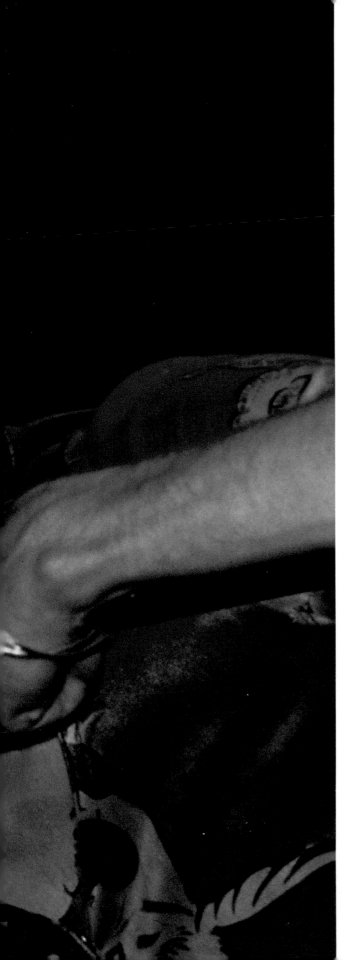

who recognized the romance of rock performance as theater, Bowie became a leader. He exposed the rock persona as a self-created role, a fantasy to be reshaped at will. Moreover, his glittering futuristic visions weren't the cotton candy of the sweet teen idols and of Broadway, but were nightmares shared by credible fiction writers and philosophic futurists fearing disaster from inhumane technology and demagogic political leaders. Recordings like his 1972 single "Space Oddity," in which Major Tom is lost in space, and the 1974 *Diamond Dogs* album, with its theme of urban decay, of Western civilization broken down into tribes of humanoids who roam Hunger City, echoed the sentiments of poet-novelist William S. Burroughs in *Nova Express* and *The Wild Boys* as well as Doris Lessing's *Survivor.*

Bowie's act had an element in common with performance artists and avant-garde figures of the music theater, including Robert Wilson, Robert Ashley, and Meredith Monk, all of whom offer highly stylized pageants of image and song instead of naturalistic psychological representations. However, when these artists, like their aesthetic forebears Bertold Brecht and Kurt Weill, made the performed song the basis of their theater, success depended on a sophisticated audience aware of irony in artifice. Bowie's viewers generally lacked such awareness, and even some journalists failed to see beyond his grease paint and images of gender-bending. But Bowie extended the performance beyond the theater stage, even getting his friends Lou Reed and Iggy Pop to play along in press conference

David Bowie as Ziggy Stardust, 1972–73

theatrics, which involved kissing each other and Bowie's wife Angela biting the breast of a female journalist. Despite his multiple image changes, fans appeared to believe in the congruence of the person with the painted persona. Nevertheless, Bowie used costume the way many artists use paint on canvas, to construct figures in fantasy landscapes.

*D*avid Bowie, The Man Who Sold the World *album cover, 1971*

David Bowie was a self-creation in the tradition of Elvis Presley, who also developed a series of public images—though more slowly than Bowie did. Bowie joined rock bands in high school and was reputed to wear his hair in what was called an "elephant's trunk," in which the sides were slicked back into the Elvis ducktail and the top was combed forward to form a "trunk." (In America, this style was also known as "the banana.") The rest of his outfit was taken from trendy Mod fashion. But also central to Mod dressing was the use of make-up on males, including lipstick, cheek color, eye shadow,

and powder. Although Bowie had a series of unsuccessful single songs when he styled himself after the British pop singer Anthony Newley in the late sixties, he also studied with mime Lindsay Kemp and dabbled in Buddhism in 1967. Years later, in 1979, he was to say to the press, "I was David Jones from Britain who wanted to do something artistically worthwhile. But I hadn't the courage to face the audience as myself."

During a 1970 visit to America he was introduced to Andy Warhol and Lou Reed of the Velvet Underground just before Reed launched his solo career. Upon returning home, Bowie worked with Marc Bolan in Bolan's progressive rock phase, before Bolan's group, Tyrannosaurus Rex, had a string of pop singles. Finally, by 1971, Bowie had formulated his own early version of the glam rocker on the cover of his album *The Man Who Sold the World*. He draped himself on a couch in a parody of a Pre-Raphaelite painting by Dante Gabriel Rosetti, wearing a floral dress and bleached blond locks, falling below shoulder level. This cover was changed to a nondescript cartoon for American consumption, so few in the United States ever saw the costume. Bowie also promoted the album in England by wearing some of his wife Angie's dresses in public. The album sold very well there, and the next one, *Hunky Dory*, maintained the androgyne image in a dress but cropped the photograph above the chest to produce a more ambiguous image.

With his 1972 album and tour, *The-Rise-and-Fall of Ziggy Stardust and the Spiders from Mars*, Bowie moved from ordinary transsexual dressing to science fiction with glamour elements.

The Ziggy Stardust character was supposedly a combination of cartoon science fiction and the legend of a rock star. This time the glamour was more alien than feminine. Bowie's friend Freddy Buretti created the outfits from ideas and images Bowie suggested. It is said that Ziggy's spiky, carrot-red hairdo came from a fashion photo in *Vogue* magazine. Ziggy often wore a mimelike white base make-up, with color added on top. Skin-tight jumpsuits in a variety of stripes, checks, and solid colors, with built-out shoulders modeled on Buck Rogers-type space suits, and platform boots made him a sort of futuristic harlequin. These outfits alternated with a white satin suit. The Spiders behind Ziggy wore red and platinum sequins on their suits. Ziggy and the Spiders opened their tops to the waist and wore knee-high, lace-up platform boots. In the album, Ziggy visits earth's dying civilization and becomes the messianic figure of salvation. Unfortunately, the album and tour coincided with the release of the science fiction social satire film *Clockwork Orange,* in which street violence accompanies the decaying society. Taking their cue from the film, Bowie's fans also went delinquent and began to spray-paint slogans like "Bowie is Ziggy, Ziggy is God." The image was so powerful that, even after he dropped the Ziggy costume, fans persisted in imitating it, sometimes for years afterward.

Ziggy was a cartoon caricature of what social and literary critic Roland Barthes, in *Mythologies,* called the "jet-man," who belongs to a myth of a celestial race. The jet-man is principally recognized by his appearance: "racial apartness can be read in his morphology: the anti-G suit of inflatable nylon,

the shiny helmet, introduce the jet-man into a novel type of skin in which *'even his mother would not know him.'* We are dealing with a true racial conversion, all the more credible since science fiction has already largely substantiated this metamorphosis of species." Barthes also noted in the jet-man elements of Parsifal, the grail-seeking hero.

Joseph Campbell's *Hero with a Thousand Faces* states that the medieval story from which Richard Wagner created his opera *Parsifal* represented social conventions as obstacles to the hero's salvation. Every departure from the "law" was a creative act, because there is no fixed law or established knowledge of god that can attain for one the spiritual grail. Only love supplies the possibility of a grail vision. Precisely such themes of rebellion and exalted love are the stuff of many rock lyrics. Bowie's Ziggy combined two powerful mythic images: the androgynous young spiritual Paraclete with the messianic spaceman. It was impossible to replace this figure with another stage character of equal potency.

The photographic cover of David Bowie's 1973 *Aladin Sane* (a pun on "a lad insane") album shows a graphic red-and-blue lightning bolt extending from Bowie's left forehead to his right cheek, over a magenta and pink make-up base. Perhaps symbolizing schizophrenia, the lightning-riven image was said to have come from a development of Ziggy, identification with the mental illness of Bowie's brother, and a feeling about rock 'n' roll America. During his tour of Japan to promote the album, he commissioned fashion designer Kansai Yamamoto (who had previously given Bowie a cos-

tume that snapped from neck to crotch and could be popped off in one blow) to create nine outfits based on traditional Japanese drama. They ranged from tight-clinging pieces, such as a striped, one-legged suit of beaded tights with a set of doughnutlike rings and a green feather boa, to others such as a ballooning cape and bell-bottom pants with cuffed bottoms nearly three feet wide. In addition to these, he also donned a near-nude sumo-wrestler-type outfit and learned new make-up techniques from Japan's popular Kabuki star Tomasu Boro.

Bowie used a different set of costumes for Western audiences in the 1973 television show "The Midnight Special," performed at the Marquee Club in London and videotaped for American broadcast. The costumes ranged from a red plastic corset with two large black feathers stretching from his waist up past his ears, to fishnetting with lamé hands over his chest (hands on his groin area were censored), to a simple black jock strap revealing a bit of pubic hair. After this, Bowie dropped the glam androgyne.

His image in 1974 and 1975 was that of a thin white duke in flat shoes, gray suit with pleated pants, and skulls and ropes as props. He performed on a bare stage with white lights, which were intended to make him look like a black-and-white photographic representation taken from pre-Hitler Berlin. By 1977 he veered toward the clown and hired Natasha Kornilof to design a humorous set of entertaining outfits. She recounted how they worked together: "We had torn bits of magazines and we did small drawings. We had lots of ideas and he wanted

David Bowie, 1973

trousers that were kind of big to combine with Hawaiian jackets (those funny shirts that they used to wear in the '40s), the ones with strange prints on them." They combined a funny mess jacket with large trousers, a series of velour track suits with a snakeskin jacket over them and lots of corduroy, hats, and sailor suits.

While touring outfits require a certain durable practicality and mass appeal, video performances can offer more of the fantastic surreal because they are supported by dreamlike background montages and fast cutting from scene to scene and shot to shot. What might not work onstage for an extended period of time can be greatly enjoyed for less than thirty seconds. In his "Ashes to Ashes" video, Bowie becomes—among other things—a *pagliaccio* clown with mime make-up right out of the commedia dell'arte, while in "The Boys Keep Swinging," the three women in lamé gowns and shoulder fins are Bowie himself.

After he dropped the glitter image, he played "good guys" in such nonsinging films as *The Man Who Fell to Earth*, *The Hunger*, and *Merry Christmas, Mr. Lawrence*. Although his costumes in these films were undeniably male, the characters were vulnerable martyrs with androgynous overtones. Most recently, in his 1986 musical-performance films, Bowie plays the "bad guy." *Absolute Beginners*, derived from Colin MacInnes's tale of the British pop scene, implies (unlike the book) that record industry investment in real estate prompted London's 1950s race riots by paying Teddy Boys to harass blacks. Bowie, singing in conservative business suit and short hair, plays the evil executive who

tempts the innocent young hero. In another 1986 film, *Labyrinth*, a combination puppet-animation and human performance fantasy for children, Bowie plays the king of goblins in ersatz medieval garb. He becomes a high fantasy character, who tries alternately to seduce and punish the teen heroine. Ellis Flyte created Bowie's costumes for *Labyrinth*.

Although animated cartoons are already a staple in music video, *Labyrinth*'s use of advanced, large-scale puppetry integrates a compelling dream dimension into live music performance within a physically tangible space in a way that other combinations of graphic and electronic animation have not (because they always break down as a juxtaposition or superimposition of one medium upon another). If this collaboration of performance arts continues to be explored in rock music, perhaps we can look forward to costume and creatures of increasingly expanded degrees of imagination and creativity freed from naturalistic

convention, which will exist within cohesive supernatural worlds. Music videos have already broken out of the narrative conventions of present science fiction and fantasy formats. It remains for collaborations of performers, costume designers, puppeteers, and filmmakers to forge more extended visions that go beyond the vaudeville entertainment tradition. Bowie and his collaborators have explored such an expansion of the rock 'n' roll theater of romance.

As for the rest of the glitter rockers of the late seventies, few have survived into the eighties. Young fans appeared to find that androgynous glitter no longer assuaged their frustrations and anger. They turned to heavy metal and punk rock, which asserted very aggressive confrontational stances. However, metalists adapted glamour elements, and the punkers took great care in stylization of their costumes to separate themselves visually from ordinary dress. Both carried on the legacy of theatrical dressing.

*D*avid Bowie, 1972, and from the
Ashes to Ashes *single and video, 1978*

Dionysus Electrified

HEAVY METAL ROCK

Shunned by radio, knocked by critics, and abhorred by all but its diehard fans as the last rats' nest of terminally untalented sexist pigs, heavy metal music sells and sells and sells. The look is frenzy by design, the act is destruction by sound, and the targeted audience is no older than eighteen. Heavy metal is the ear-splitting rock anthem of adolescent rebellion, which proclaims partying to the loudest sounds as the height of liberation. On its darker side, it is the most visual and vociferous of all rock in its glorification of misogyny, violence, death, satanism, and plain old-fashioned insanity. Its apotheosis of ecstasy in all forms recalls rites of the ancient cults of Dionysus with his savage followers.

Heavy metal is rock 'n' roll on the scale of

Gene Simmons, 1985

acoustical and visual outrage. Its performances are the loudest, most anarchic, and most feared by parents, concert promoters, and the police because its devotees tend to try to destroy everything in sight during and after a concert. Its musicians onstage wield their axes as weapons one moment and as phallic symbols the next amid grand stage sets, mountains of speakers, lasers, and smoke. Aficionados of metal music, known as "headbangers" for their insistent up-and-down head motion in time to the thundering beat, typically show appreciation for a great show by throwing firecrackers and bottles, ripping out seats, and indulging in "stage diving"—mounting the stage and leaping off into the crowd.

Defined as a separate rock genre in the late 1960s, heavy metal first peaked in 1973, nearly expired by 1980, and since then has risen like the

Motley Crüe, dressed by Fleur Thiemeyer, 1985

phoenix from its ashes while splintering into several substyles of sound and costume. The music press adopted the name, describing the late-sixties mixture of electric blues and acid rock, from the 1968 Steppenwolf song "Born to Be Wild," which used the phrase "heavy metal thunder," quoted from William Burroughs's book *Naked Lunch*.

Metal's extreme amplification and deliberate electronic tonal distortions include ecstatic high-frequency guitar screeches and other synthetic emissions loud enough to rebound off the walls of the largest arenas. Melody and lyrics rank low in importance, and driving rhythm high. Rock historians track its aural precedents to Link Wray's 1958 single hit "Rumble," which featured "fuzzy" sound produced by a pencil poked into one of the instrument amplifier's speakers. For establishing "fuzz tone" as basic to hard rock, other authorities credit the Kinks' 1964 British number-one single "You Really Got Me," the Yardbirds' 1965 "Shape of Things to Come," the Who's 1966 "My Generation," and the acid rock of Jimi Hendrix and the Jefferson Airplane between 1967 and 1968.

But the first group to distinguish itself with

a distinctly metal attitude was California's Blue Cheer. Their 1968 album *Vincebus Eruptum* and their stage act had a ponderous, pseudo-Gothic flavor, which is the cornerstone of the heavy metal sound, attitude, and imagery. Other 1969 albums solidified the style (for example: MC5's *Kick Out the Jams*, Grand Funk Railroad's *Heavy*, Black Pearl's *Black Pearl*, the Stooges' *The Stooges*, and Mountain's *Mountain*). Now the visual aspect of the performance started to become as important as the music. Legend has it that the Stooges sometimes flayed the flesh off themselves onstage, and that their leader, Iggy Pop, would rake nails across his bare chest to draw blood. The Stooges were reputed to "empty a house quicker than any fire alarm." Yet metalists became idols to teens despite—or perhaps because of—adverse musical and parental criticism. Rock critic Henry Edwards wrote in the early seventies that, "Just ten seconds into the first cut on my new Black Sabbath album *Master of Reality*, my bathtub drain miraculously unclogged itself for the first time in three months." Nonetheless, in the first three years of the seventies, such metalists as Black Sabbath, Deep Purple, Alice Cooper, Blue Öyster Cult, Kiss, Aerosmith, and Led Zeppelin played the most popular type of rock. In 1970, Led Zeppelin even displaced the Beatles as the number-one rock group in England, and in 1975 the group had six albums on the British top 100 pop chart at once.

Then, temporarily diminished by disco's *Saturday Night Fever* glamour and punk rock's even tougher, more alienated stance, metal split into two main visual categories, thrash metal and glam rock and a host of musical subdivisions such as death metal, speed metal, and a softened-up A.O.R., or adult-oriented-rock. Music television revolutionized the record industry in 1981 and pushed heavy metal veterans (some of whom were nearly two decades older than their fans) as well as newcomers to fame. Examples of the thrashers include Judas Priest, Iron Maiden, Ozzy Osbourne, Venom, and Motorhead. Their costumes descend from the Gene Vincent tradition of black leather jackets and jeans. The glam contingent, rooted in early seventies glitter rock, includes such examples as Kiss, Motley Crüe, Ratt, and Quiet Riot (and Ozzy Osbourne in the mid 1980s).

Metal's look of transgression generally upsets adults more than their sound and aggressive lyrics do—although adults usually have no affection for these either. The performers strive to look larger than life, with costumes that transform them into stylized characters out of horror comics. Accessories include massive coiffures with woven-in hair extensions or wigs, which look as electrified as their guitars, high heels (formerly platform boots, but now updated with Cuban heels), sadomasochistic paraphernalia, glittery Spandex with large cut-out holes, and leather studded with spikes and nail heads. Additional details, from the psychedelic era, linger in headbands, colored scarves, logo t-shirts, fringes, and jewelry for men. In the late 1970s and early 1980s a bit of punk, with its torn garments, was integrated into glam and metal's grafting of mucho-macho motorcycle garb of leather and chains onto the flower-power image of anarchy and ecstasy to produce a new hybrid outlaw who was more offensive to middle-class values than any of the individual factions by themselves. Such a rebellious visual combination was bound to sell, for it has become almost formulaic that anything their parents hate is what teens go wild for—at least temporarily. But unlike most fads, heavy metal did not disappear, for it offered what no other culturally sanctioned source could—the ceremony, message, and costume of religion without the tears and guilt.

CRISES IN THE SEVENTIES

After a 1970 mass-market survey discovered that thirteen-to-seventeen-year-olds accounted for 81 percent of all popular record sales, music companies lost no time marketing products aimed at this group. Young female teens ate up the industry-originated "pube rock" of the Monkees (a Beatles imitation), the Osmond Brothers, and David Cassidy. Like most synthetically manufactured fads, these bubblegum pop stars disappeared as quickly as the Hula Hoop. By contrast, adolescent males went for metal music rooted in basic mythic images.

The blossoming of heavy metal from 1969 to 1973 accompanied youthful disillusionment and retreat into the seventies "me" decade. Nineteen sixty-nine saw Nixon begin his second term with Cambodian bombings while anti-Vietnam War demonstrations ignited 448 colleges and universities. The draft was picking off all who could not attend college. Woodstock was over, and in 1970 Nixon invaded Cambodia; Kent State University students were killed by National Guard bullets, and rock stars Jimi Hendrix and Janis Joplin fatally overdosed on drugs. Jim Morrison of the Doors, Brian Jones of the Rolling Stones, and Duane Allman of the Allman Brothers Band died, and the Beatles broke up. The teen's heroes were gone.

The seventies also mass-popularized the occult. In 1970 the First Festival of the Occult Arts assembled at the Fillmore East in Manhattan, while the University of California at Berkeley offered the first academic credits for "Magical Studies." Occult literature and posters were standard in head shops established to sell psychedelic paraphernalia. In 1972 "Jesus Freaks" became the latest youth movement, and Pan American Airlines offered the $629 package "Psychic Tour" of Britain, which included a seance and a day at Stonehenge with the "Chief Druid." Heavy metal music simply mirrored the times with Led Zeppelin's 1971 hit "Stairway to Heaven" and their album *Led Zeppelin IV* (the "runes album"), which blended post-hippie mysticism, mythological preoccupations, and hard rock. Their leader-songwriter Jimmy Page's fascination with Celtic lore evoked a pseudo-religious aura, which became a feature of metal imagery.

THE GOSPEL ACCORDING TO HEAVY METAL

When philosopher T. E. Hulme scorned romanticism as spoiled religion too cowardly to take dogma straight, his definition might well have encompassed metal's pop romance with the occult, ecstasy, and satanism. Satisfying teen rebellion against authority, metal's look and lyrics assuage youthful forebodings of personal chaos and rationalize antisocial urges. Themes of imminent apocalypse (e.g., Iron Maiden's "Two Minutes to Midnight," or Rush's "Distant Early Warning"), damnation (e.g., Grim Reaper's "See You in Hell,"

Slayer's "Hell Awaits"), and insanity (e.g., Quiet Riot's "Mama, We're All Crazee Now," the Killer Dwarfs' "Heavy Metal Breakdown," or Anthrax's "Madhouse") outweigh themes of optimism. Death is entertainment, and let's go down partying is a key message. Iron Maiden combs lyrics from the Bible and mythology in their search for foreboding images of war (as in their "The Trooper" and "Run to the Hills"). Seven of the eight cuts from their 1982 album *The Number of the Beast* pertain to death, and the group's main stage prop was a ten-foot-high rotting corpse. Motley Crüe, a glam metal group, used the pentagram sign of Satan as a band symbol. The tattered look, with holes in shirts and pants and torn-off strips of fake animal fur (usually zebra, tiger, or leopard), came partially from punk rock. They may have taken inspiration from the two popular cult films, *The Road Warrior* of 1982 and its sequel in 1985, *Mad Max Beyond Thunderdome*. Norma Moriceaux, who designed the costumes for both of these films, expanded the iconography of the British punk look to include the mythic images of the American Indian with Mohawk haircut and the 1950s leather-clad biker. Her international costume hybrid, in turn, influenced rock performances and street fashion of the early and mid 1980s. The apocalypse themes of these films, like those of heavy metal and also of Lessing's *Survivor* and Burroughs's *The Wild Boys*, feature roving bands of raggedy teens dominating what is left of civilization.

*B*ruce Dickinson of
Iron Maiden, 1984. Francine Hunter of Jungle Red
Studios in a Burghard Schmidt design, 1982

Although heavy metal stage costumes often incorporate swastikas, crosses, and Celtic or Nordic imagery, the archetypal role model here, in two respects, is Dionysus. First, metal's celebration of intoxicated partying recalls Greek Dionysian cult revels known as the "Ambrosia," in which the satyrs (goat-totem tribesmen), centaurs (horse-totem tribesmen), and their Maenads (women) used wine to wash down mouthfuls of *amanita muscaria,* a hallucinatory mushroom. Ambrosia was the secret element of the Eleusian, Orphic, and all other mysteries associated with Dionysus. Second, the ritual slaying and rebirth of this divinity each year connected him with death cults. In addition to some cannibalism, Dionysian mystery rites before the fifth century culminated in ripping apart animals and human beings.

Glam metal's fey obsession with profuse adornment, elaborate coiffures, Spandex, sequins, and colorful make-up also recalls the mythic effeminacy of the divine debauchee (Dionysus' acquired female mannerisms were rationalized in myth by the tale of his isolated upbringing by the nymphs of Nysa—female, of course). Hair emporiums catering to rock performers advertise their expertise in creating the voluminous manes typical of metalists. Zario of "After Six" described the three basic methods of hair extension: weaving natural and synthetic hair into one's own locks (the ends of which are secured with something like Krazy Glue); clip-on extensions, which attach via comblike fasteners near one's own roots; and new, improved custom wigs, guaranteed not to come off even when swimming. 1986 prices for extra stage hair ran from $3 for a "spark" clip-in swatch of "Kanelon" acrylic, to $1,800 for a wig made from a cast mold of one's scalp. Woven-in extensions also can run into the hundreds of dollars and require "ventilation" touch-ups every four weeks as one's own hair grows. It also appears obligatory for metalists to present at least one (if not more) band members with bleached platinum locks, while other partners often dye theirs black for the greatest theatrical contrast. An advantage of being a blond on stage and on video is that back lighting these frizzed-out tresses creates a halo around the head. *Voila*—instant holiness. A homelier reason for enhancing tresses is that the balding and graying of many metal performers, in their thirties pushing forty, requires cosmetic rejuvenation to retain youthful credibility.

Make-up, hair coloring, and elaborate coiffures for men still fall within the macho rock tradition. Elvis himself resorted to black hair dye and mascara to heighten his dark good looks when he returned to the stage after the army. Little Richard, although no dream of the American he-man, also got away with heavy pancake make-up, mascara, and his infamous six-inch high pompadour—decades before rock made glitter okay. Before metal, male entertainers who weren't trying to appear androgynous aimed to enhance their own assets. By contrast, metalist face paint is both flamboyantly artificial and also supposed to be virile, 100 percent straight male. If there are any doubts, one can note the number of tattoos on metalists' bodies—sure evidence of a manly ability to withstand pain.

Tattoos, so prominent on many metal rockers, such as Ozzy Osbourne, Iron Maiden's Steve

Harris, the late Bon Scott of AC/DC, Stephen Pearcy of Ratt, Peter Criss formerly of Kiss, and all of the Motley Crüe, have their counterpart in myth. The Cyclopses, who were depicted in myth as one-eyed giants, were actually early Helladic bronze smiths who tattooed their foreheads with concentric circles in honor of the sun. The tattoo may have been described as a giant eye. Although now viewed as macho decoration, tattooing was once executed out of fear of disaster to ward off evil, prolong life, prevent disease, and stand the bearers of these religious marks in good stead on Judgment Day. So many Irish monks and pilgrims to the Holy Land received holy designs that a church council in Northumberland, England, banned the practice in A.D. 787. Seen as the "Mark of Cain" by Jewish orthodoxy, tattoos signaled outcasts from society. Colonial pilgrims in this country also frowned upon the Native American practice of sacred tattooing. Such animadversions notwithstanding, wealthy socialite women in the United States started a tattoo fad near the turn of the century, a kind of exotic naughtiness that lasted into the nineteen-teens. Between the sailor, the saint, and the debutante, metallist tattoos variously evoke associations of religion, magic, and rebellion.

As their costumes have become more stylized, band members look less and less like their audience, who wear jeans, sneakers, t-shirts, and denim or leather jackets. The more unnatural and apart from ordinary life the bands appear, the more they approach images of the supernatural. However, fans' hair has gotten a bit wilder. Female headbangers dress like the boys or the vampy cheesecake sirens featured on their heroes' rock videos.

COURTESY TRIPP NYC

Heavy-metal-influenced fashion, 1985

THE ORIGINATORS

Although the majority of metal rock costumes now seem to be cloned by formula, a few historic innovators set precedents that inspired hordes of imitators. Alice Cooper, Kiss, and Judas Priest were exemplary of three archetypal costume approaches in this area: the ghoul, the stylized "glam" artist, and the sadomasochistic thrasher.

Alice Cooper's willingness to act and dress as disgustingly as possible upped the shock-tolerance ante in rock. His appearance and stage antics so

119

overshadowed his music that the latter is scarcely mentioned in rock chronicles, while every account details the rest of his act. Cooper's 1971 rock theater of the grotesque featured a live boa constrictor, giant spiders and vampires, guillotine, dolls, and macabre make-up. Cooper, naked to the waist and clad in black leather pants, boots, garish lipstick, eyeshadow, and a Dracula-of-Drag French-twist hairstyle, would cut off dolls' heads, twine his snake about his body and kiss it, and simulate rites of cannibalism with his rubber babies. A decade later, Ozzy Osbourne, who also performed part of his stage act naked from the waist up, repeated a part of the act by biting off the head of a live dove on stage. A year later, in 1982, Osbourne also bit into what he thought was a fake bat, which a fan had tossed to him during a Des Moines, Iowa, show. He was rushed to the hospital for a painful series of rabies shots. Cooper deliberately placed himself in danger with such performance gambits as "Can Alice Cooper Escape the Cage of Fire?" Confined within a flaming enclosure from which he could not escape until it burned down, he reported that it nearly roasted him like a "Bavarian shish kebab," but "it was a great effect." His autobiography explains that he made the cage for fifteen dollars, with bent shower rods and forty to fifty loosely rolled plastic bags hung at different levels around the frame. The rest of his group played music while the burning plastic coagulated in fiery balls, which fell to the ground around him, emitting loud *whssts*. When club owners billed him for damage for their burned

*A*lice Cooper, 1977; Welcome to My Nightmare *tour, 1976–77*

stages, he switched to an oversized electric chair with thick leather straps and metal skull plate, complete with electrodes. While the costume components on his body weren't as original as his stage props, his urgent striving to make himself appear ghoulish in them established an aesthetic of deliberate ugliness as teen rebellion. At the time it may have seemed extraordinary that such an act sold so well. Yet kids have long thrived on monster comics and horror films. Cooper transferred the thrill of dread from other media to the rock concert stage.

Beginning in 1973, Kiss was pivotal in transforming hard rock into pure show biz. Although their music was scoffed at by critics as pedestrian, their flair for showmanship, the pure fantasy of extraterrestrial outfits, and total-face Kabuki make-up meshed with simple lyrics geared to adolescent concerns to propel them to the top of the concert circuit. Playing amid stage smoke, explosions, and hydraulic lifts, Kiss so captured the youth audience that they were featured in a television cartoon and two Marvel Comics in 1977. Their costume designer, Larry LeGaspi, made a composite image from animal, science fiction, glitter rock, and Oriental sources. He molded the boot covers in clay over platform shoes and cast these forms in Kybex plastic, built body suits studded with rhinestones and nail heads, and cut and layered leather scallops into platelets for armor. The intricate outfits were most definitely beyond the financial means or craft skills of local garage bands imitating their heroes. Ace Frehley wore exaggerated shaped and trapunto-

Ozzy Osbourne, dressed by Fleur Thiemeyer, 1986

corded silver Lurex flying shoulder wings, waist-, wrist-, and armbands on his rhinestone-studded top and Lurex-quilted platform-boot coverings, which came to the knees of his skin-tight Spandex pants. Gene Simmons's scaled leather platelet armor over his arms and upper torso, and over-the-knee plat-

Fleur Thiemeyer sketch for Ozzy Osbourne, 1986

form boots, Peter Criss's elaborate sequined jumpsuit, and Paul Stanley's feathered coat all required superb professional craftsmanship. The only things that indigent fans could do was to don the theatrical make-up, which Kiss members wore for every public appearance from 1973 to 1981. But daily imitation was impractical, since full-face make-up on males obviously would not sit well at school. No matter how great the adulation, Kiss's outfits could have little direct impact on teen fashion. On the other hand, their outright dismissal of naturalism influenced such eighties heavy metalists as Ratt, Motley Crüe, Twisted Sister, and others who use heavily

The original Kiss, dressed by Larry LeGaspi, 1972

styled artifice emphasizing a kind of other-worldly fantasy.

When heavy metal sales dropped around 1981, Kiss wiped off their make-up, reformed their group with two new members, and began to revamp

their image. They commissioned costume designer Fleur Thiemeyer, who built them separates with strategically cut holes in Spandex, and t-shirts with stitched and laced-on net, zebra and leopard skin strips and patches, plus leather wristlets, straps, and wide belts. In 1986, Thiemeyer again redesigned their costumes to add more color, glamour, and flowing fabric.

Judas Priest, an English band, which has been together since 1971 and popular since 1977, at first explicitly exemplified the sadomasochistic metal costume. Their leader and singer, Rob Halford, a thirty-five-year-old actor-dropout, first formulated the exaggerated leather look with studs, chains, and bondage accessories that he bought in shops carrying S&M gear. Priest's leathers would scarcely blend in with the Hell's Angels pig look, for the stage outfits had a designer cast, with so much metal ornamentation that Halford mocked his own stage entrance, which was announced by the loud jangling of much hardware, saying, "One day they'll have to bring me out in a wheelbarrow." Unlike the majority of metal musicians, Halford has not adopted the post-hippie shag coiffure with hair extensions. His rather severely cropped platinum tresses evoke the sinister look of a disciplined S.S. officer instead of the frizzed-out, let-it-all-hang-loose, fuzz top ubiquitous with other metalists. Although the rest of his band sport longer lengths, their styling lacks the elaborate teasing and processing that makes white musicians look like Africans *manqué*. Whatever stage make-up Judas Priest wears, it is not prominent to the video eye—a striking contrast to those who lay it on thickly. The look is that of a clean machine, impersonal in the sense of appearing remote from human vulnerability, omnipotent and authoritarian.

During the early eighties, Judas Priest began to shift its image and stage performance toward science fiction. Whereas in the late seventies Halford sang atop a black Harley-Davidson low-rider cycle, with raised clenched fists and brandishing a riding crop, while the guitar duo of K. K. Downing and Glenn Tipton crossed their guitars in the air to form a crucifix, now he has a chrome-plated cycle with an animal-head front. He also has performed with a robot onstage. Costume designer Ray Brown has developed art-deco-influenced costumes from a lightweight synthetic leather, which gives a streamlined look of modernity. This 1986 image has been christened "heavy deco." From 1982 until this year, Mr. Brown was the only designer to make rock costumes from this totally washable and dry-cleanable, lightweight Japanese fabric (which he declines to name specifically). It stretches in use but goes back into shape with washing, and it is stronger than leather (wet leather rips under stress). Here the costume materials of high technology match the musicians' stage imagery and endure the hardships of stage activity.

After 1981 the rigid heavy metal signature colors of black and silver gave way to black, red, and white, and finally to the whole spectrum. Ray Brown's 1986 deco outfits for Judas Priest have (according to the designer) twenty hues, ranging from gold and silver to black and purple. Among other

*R*ob Halford of Judas Priest, 1985

*D*ee Snider and Twisted Sister, 1985

groups there has also been a softening of the mis-ogynist posturing, and romantic pirate blouson shirting and chiffon have appeared. Women have also been included for the first time in metal music, while blacks—except for Znowhite—are conspic-uously absent among performers and are rare in metal audiences.

In the mid 1970s maverick Ted Nugent dis-tinguished his image by standing apart in his noble savage outfit, consisting of only a tiny loin cloth and his exuberantly waved tawny tresses flowing down to

his nipples. As an androgynous Tarzan, he became a male heir to Tina Turner's skimpy jungle queen and tribal goddess costume imagery of the 1960s. By the 1980s he was wearing pants but remained naked to the waist.

Ronnie James Dio, formerly of Black Sab-bath and Rainbow, has turned the heavy metal dun-geon into Camelot for the youngest headbangers. His medieval-styled laced jerkin, shield, and sword look less like glam or thrash than something out of Tolkien's fantasy trilogy. Thor combines comic-strip

*J*udas Priest, dressed by Ray Brown, 1986

Viking garb with Buck Rogers video plots for a blend of science fiction, medieval, and thrasher fantasy in "Knock 'Em Down."

By contrast, Angus Young, guitarist with the Australian AC/DC, a group recording from the mid 1970s into the 1980s, has preserved a light touch with his schoolboy's uniform of short pants, crested school blazer, white shirt, white socks, wide striped tie, and tiny visored hat. However, the outfit has had nothing particularly to do with the group's lyrics; rather, it has registered as a gimmick to distinguish

Young visually from the rest of the band, who wear jeans, t-shirts, and roadster hats with front visor brims and eight-piece circular crowns.

THE CLOWNS

Dionysian frenzy is often replaced by humor that scorches authority. In Heaven's video "Rock School" and Motley Crüe's "Smokin' in the Boy's Room," the singers caricature high school principals and teachers, triumphing over them through the power of their music. Raven's video "On and On" plots their battle

with the ridiculous-looking staff of Creepy Records, and Ozzy Osbourne's "Zero the Hero" features all characters with grotesque ghoulish scars and wigs in a Frankenstein take-off.

David Lee Roth combines roles of sex symbol and clown in such videos as Van Halen's 1984 "Hot for Teacher," and, in his solo career, with "Just a Gigolo" and "Yankee Rose." The first featured him as bus driver, schoolboy, and pop singer—with a parody of the Temptations/Four Tops look-and-dance-alike routine—and a quiz show announcer. The second satirized other music stars, such as Willie Nelson, Boy George, Michael Jackson, and others, which Roth parodies in their characteristic costumes. The 1986 "Yankee Rose" features Roth as a sexy, silly, madcap harlequin doing a bump and wiggle act inside a glittering Spandex jumpsuit, with large graphic stripes and circle patterns, and a pair of seatless pants with a rear tail flap.

Dee Snider, male lead singer for Twisted Sister, was named to a 1984 list of worst-dressed women and was described as looking like a bad dream at Mardi Gras. Instead of appearing ghoulish in the Alice Cooper vein, he looked ridiculous. The band originally salvaged their costumes from the fat ladies' section of department stores and then annihilated these pieces before they put them on. Snider was their campy focal point, with his wild corkscrew curls down past his shoulders, ragged, fringed separates, and heavily painted face with a signature sneer. Although now cleaned up and appearing more glam than slam and at the peak of their fame, in

*W*endy O. Williams, 1982

1982 they were viewed by rock critics as a hopeless anachronism confined to the Tri-state East Coast bar circuit because their visual and musical style was based on such seventies performers as Cooper, Black Sabbath, Led Zeppelin, Slade, and the New York Dolls. But like Jimi Hendrix, who was first ignored in his native land, adulation during their foreign tour propelled them to fame.

METAL WOMEN

Heavy metal has been openly misogynist in lyrics and videos, and record companies offered hard-rocking women no record contracts until the late 1970s. Directed at pubescent, frustrated white males unsure of their sexual identity, metal's heterosexual aggression against women was acceptable to fans who felt that unavailable women deserved punishment. The all-maleness of metal was simply more open and honest in its antifeminism than the softer rock genres, which sometimes had a female singer fronting a performance or record. In the past, to break into metal as a composer-performer, a woman had to become "one of the boys."

Lita Ford, Joan Jett and the Blackhearts, and Wendy O. Williams with the Plasmatics wore the obligatory thrasher look, while Girlschool dons a version of the glam patchwork-and-Spandex uniform. Lee Aaron, of Metal Queen, performs the whole S&M dungeon-swordplay-boa-constrictor-imprisonment-in-chains scene in leather miniskirt and studded accessories. Precious Metal substitutes the sarong miniskirt for the standard Spandex pants but copies the gents in most other paraphernalia. The Plasmatics' mid-1980s videos exaggerate the

Lita Ford, 1985

Sturm und Drang destructive aspect so heavily that the scenario becomes comic. Long known for their act, which involves the annihilation of various objects, Williams continues the schtick on "The Damned," video. Clad in a bleached, spiked-up Mohawk hairstyle, studded gauntlets and boots, bikini, and dangling chains from her wide leather belt, Wendy O. Williams drives a school bus into a mountain of television sets, which explode into

flames on contact. Of course, she survives with nary a hair out of place. In "It's My Life," again donning leather straps and studs, she plays a variety of macho roles, from woman wrestler fighting in the ring, to wrecking a house, and climbing out of a speeding car onto the dangling ladder of a helicopter flying overhead. Her car then speeds over a cliff and explodes, as she is hoisted away.

Whether by choice or by record company

130

encouragement, metalist women conform to standard looks set by males. Although earlier female hard rockers, like Janis Joplin and Patti Smith, developed highly individual images, they were solo stars with back-up bands. But heavy metal is a group form, in which team bonding is emphasized and personal individuation is subservient to the whole. Having been barred from the club both as women and as individuals, their best possible route to original imagery would seem to be finding different mythic archetypes that show themselves as goddesses in their own right rather than groupie/Maenad followers of Dionysus. New wave women rockers have done just that.

Girlschool, 1985

131

Punk to New Wave Fashion

Punk, if treated with extreme delicacy and sensibility, can be made to work with this season's overall fashion direction. Take the torn T-shirt. Carefully slashed to ribbons, it can work perfectly with freshly minted blue jeans and a wool overshirt. Worn as part of an overall Punk statement, however, it's unsubtle.

Peter Carlson, fashion editor of GQ *Magazine, "Portrait in Black,"* GQ, *October 1977*

Just back from a trip to America, Rhodes [Zandra Rhodes, British fashion designer] says she heard customers in Bloomingdale's saying they couldn't wait to wear Punk on nightclub crawls. "And I dress quite straight ladies."

American stores, in addition to Bloomingdale's, which have bought Punk are Giorgio's in Beverly Hills, and Marie Leavell in Dallas, Rhodes says. She also reports some hefty orders from Germany, and she is now doing her best to speed up deliveries. Meanwhile, Eydie Gorme wore two of Rhodes' Punk outfits when she opened at the Palladium.

Seditionaries, the Kings Road shop which was the first to sell Punk fashions, and the originator of many of the ideas, feels Punk is just beginning to take off in a big way. So far, its bestsellers are the bondage trousers (with straps and a loin cloth) and the "God Save the Queen" T-shirt, with a photo of Her Majesty with a safety pin through her nose and mouth.

Valerie Wade, Woman's Wear Daily, *June 13, 1977*

I t's only Rock and Roll, but you wear it!" proclaimed *Woman's Wear Daily* (December 5, 1977), the bible of the New York Seventh Avenue rag trade. Thus it bestowed a blessing on punk, the first rock movement based primarily on visual style. Whereas psychedelic outfits of the sixties were originated by hippies and then co-opted by designers, the British punk look was started by designers and then undermined by real punks, who refused to be domesticated in their creations.

Shock was chic in June 1977, when Paris socialite Regine threw a party for five hundred

S id Vicious of the Sex Pistols, 1978

guests in full punk regalia. But a gang of real punks crashed the affair and caused her to call the gendarmes. The "black evening," of ready-to-wear terrorist couture staged at a punk disco called La Main Bleu, a warehouse just outside of Paris, ended in police tear gas. Never had a counterculture been so voraciously embraced, consumed, co-opted, and glamorized so quickly. Ironically, the anarchistic rock musician predecessors of the early 1970s who inspired the style took a stance of visual and musical antifashion, indeed a conservative look backward to the days of garage bands and no-frills hard rock. Yet, by 1977, punk had become an international costume party to which everyone was invited—except the original punk rockers.

The image that so entranced the fashion world was one of deprivation and self-abuse. "Sex," the boutique of British clothiers Vivienne Westwood and Malcolm McLaren, did a thriving business in 1972 selling razor-slashed t-shirts that had been sewn up again to simulate scars. They also sold t-shirts with graphic images. Such separates became fashionable with bondage chains, noses or lips pierced with safety pins, and deliberately ghoulish make-up and hairstyles. The sartorial style spread, and by 1977 the Paris shop "Survival" included such punk accessories as Japanese antipollution masks, rubber and studded gloves, and survival-food kits. The store decor featured a mannequin dripping with fake blood.

While Nazi storm trooper, bondage, and dominatrix images might have sex appeal for a few,

Johnny Rotten, 1977

this did not explain the appeal to the majority of middle- and upper-bourgeois department store and boutique customers. Indeed, for the most part, such outfits were antisexual, in that the goal of being attractive to the opposite sex was replaced by a deliberate effort to shock. Sid Vicious, of the Sex Pistols, most infamous of British punk rock bands, stated in an October 1977 *Rolling Stone* interview that he "felt like a sexless monster because at the time my head was shaved and I was wearing this vile tuxedo that was four sizes too big, I had no money to buy clothes and people would run away when I walked down the street." John Lydon, formerly Johnny Rotten of the Sex Pistols, was well aware of the link between dressing well and sexual attractiveness. "I don't mind people trying to look their best," he said in an *I-D Magazine* interview, March 1986, "I think that's a fairly healthy young thing to do—that's the pursuit of girls, isn't it? And girls don't like badly dressed idiots. I don't like clothes-horses in the music business, though." Punk costume, with its allusions to stages of utter abjection and total celibacy, may have derived its power through the unconscious quasi-religious appeal of mortification of the flesh.

THE ATTRACTION OF REPULSION

Julie Kristeva's book *The Power of Horror* details how deliberate deprivation accompanies most religiosity and is continually worked out in new guises as outworn values collapse. The ascetic, the flagellant, and the defiled find spiritual catharsis, a sense of purification that at best leads to enlightenment—or at least to reconciliation with guilt that arises from desire. While not many sane individuals would be able to justify flogging themselves for any reason, something of the hair-shirt syndrome is built into Western heritage as well as the Eastern ascetic religions. Hatred of sex was manifest in Christianity from the time of Paul, who advocated reversing the traditional Judaic morality, which required men to marry and procreate. The middle class initially hated early rock 'n' roll, which was intended to be sexy, but it was immediately magnetized by punk antireproductive references, which were imbued with Gnostic, Manichaean, and early Christian dicta, such as those of St. Augustine, to "detest our present bodies as an evil nature." The two Gnostic Christian paths to salvation were both antireproductive: asceticism and *agape*—the Love Feast orgy, in which cult members stimulated each other and then *drank* the resulting semen and also menstrual blood. Punkers weren't the first to exult in blood for an emotional lift.

The punk attitude of revulsion from the world existed in the secular Christian romance theme, which stressed commitment to social iconoclasm as an expression of mankind's homelessness in the here and now. A mystical tenet of Judaism, Christianity, and Islam viewed emotional integrity as possible only through personal union with a spiritual source of power and surviving only in opposition to social communities. Christian Gnostic sects, basing their rationale on St. Paul's pronouncement that "Christ redeemed us from the curse of laws," broke either laws of reproductive nature through severe asceticism, or else the laws of society through orgiastic celebration. According to British sociologist and rock critic Simon Firth, "punk was the first form of youth music not to rest on love songs. . . . punk interrupted the long-standing rock equation of sex and pleasure." Teens have long sought to identify with law breakers in rebellion from parental authority; but when adults with absolutely no previous connection to rock culture took up punk imagery, it was clear that some deeply emotional, if unconscious, chord had been struck.

PUNK ORIGINATORS

Perhaps the only thing that they all had in common was an aesthetic of outrage. Punk has been variously defined as a type of aggressively pounding rhythmic noise based on three-chord basics, with lyrics abounding in anger, nihilism, and alienation, with costume that revels in iconoclastic gender bending or role playing. According to these criteria, MC5, Iggy Pop and the Stooges, the Velvet Underground, the New York Dolls, and Patti Smith were the first American punks. If, however, punk is defined as a particular visual statement of dress and class antagonism, then the British Sex Pistols were there first. In practice, there rarely is any single first of any musical or visual style, but a gradual procession of individuals that finally culminates in a focused image. You can easily recognize a post-1976 punk by his or her stereotypical look and sound, whereas in the early seventies the performers were merely individual aberrations in the mainstream.

The American rock group MC5 proclaimed revolution with their 1968 debut album, *Kick Out the Jams*, in a high-energy barrage of sound. Wearing red, white, and blue glitter suits, they advocated violence, drugs, and the White Panther radical political party. They disbanded in 1972. The Tubes, popular in 1972 as a cult rock group in the San Francisco Bay Area, became known for such events as the Streakers Ball, to which all naked members of the audience were admitted free; their leather-and-chains skit, "Mondo Bondage," as well as their succession of costumes for each number; their porn film *The Resurrection of Eve*; and environmental theatrical stage design for their revue-style act. The Ramones, formed in 1974 in Forest Hills, Queens (New York), dressed in standard bad-boy torn t-shirts and black leathers, but redefined rough rock primitivism with high-decibel energetic noise and lyrics exploring such subjects as sniffing glue and being a pinhead. New Jersey-born Patti Smith, who has been called the high priestess of punk, dressed for performance in ratty t-shirts and worn boxer trunks—although her album covers presented her in garb looking more like an eighties victim of chic Japanese fashion. Despite the truly artistic, poetic bent of her lyrics, the proto-punk themes of blood and guts in "Horses," of 1975, and her personal brand of alienation in such later works as "Pissing in the River" qualified her as a leader in opposition to the cloying sweetness of the pop music sensibility. Punks were an us-against-the-world fraternity of the damned, and Patti Smith told her audience at New York's CBGB in June 1977, "Unless we keep it going, in another decade rock and roll will be art. What a shame."

By contrast, the premier British punk rock act, the Sex Pistols, was shaped by a former art student, Malcolm McLaren, and fashion designer,

Vivienne Westwood. Playing music was subsidiary to how they looked. In 1975, McLaren returned from his American debacle of trying to redesign the image of the New York Dolls, turning them into Communists by putting them into red leather and draping their stage with hammer and sickle flags. According to legend (recorded in *Rolling Stone* magazine), McLaren organized the Sex Pistols from

*T*he Tubes, ca. 1980

working-class kids hanging around his boutique who were interested in starting a band. McLaren reportedly auditioned John Lydon, the infamous Johnny Rotten, by having him stand next to the jukebox, lip-synching Alice Cooper's anthem, "I'm Eighteen." The new moniker came from a fellow member, who noticed the never-brushed ivories in the mouth of their new lead singer. In two months, the group learned to play instruments and began to perform. Rotten's incendiary anger and swastika-

CHUCK PULIN/STAR FILE

decorated t-shirt ignited the act, and his public obscenities enraged the press. Their first single, "Anarchy in the U.K.," with Rotten declaring himself an anti-Christ, became the number-one hit. Banned in most towns from performing and denounced by members of Parliament, they were still courted by record companies after EMI dropped them. In January 1976, bass player Glen Matlock quit, charging manipulation by McLaren, and Sid Vicious, who was totally inexperienced as a musician but picturesque as a bad boy, replaced him. On March 19, 1976, A&M signed the group and dropped them a week later, after the Pistols were involved in vandalizing their company headquarters and brawled in a bar with the head of programming for the BBC. By summer they re-signed with Virgin Records, released "God Save the Queen" (with the lyric, "She's no human being"), and again hit number one. Whether the band could play music or not was irrelevant, claimed Nick Lowe, member of the pre-punk bands Brinsley Schwarz and Rockpile, and who was also an acclaimed songwriter, soloist, and producer for new wave records by other artists.

And what did they think of the clothes marketed in their style? "Punk fashions are a load of bollocks. Real punks nick all their gear from junk shops," Johnny Rotten declared in the October 20, 1977 issue of *Rolling Stone*. The provocateurs who refused to become domesticated broke with McLaren in 1978 after an American tour; Sid Vicious killed his girlfriend, Nancy Spungen, and later died of a drug overdose; and the others later worked in new groups. But they also spawned a whole movement of young punk bands such as the Clash, Buzzcocks, the Damned, the Slits, and X-Ray Spexs, and also such fanzines as *Sniffin Glue*, *Ripped and Torn*, *Live Wire*, and *Chainsaw*.

Although punk primarily presented itself in masculine terms (even androgynous Patti Smith was one of the boys), such women as Poly Styrene (in X-Ray Spexs), the Slits, Siouxie Sioux, and Nina Hagen began the shift toward women in revolt as opposed to playing the role of compliant pop sex kitten. Two who lasted into the eighties, without prettifying either their lyrics or costumes were Sioux and Hagen.

Siouxie Sioux's debut at the 100 Club Punk Festival in London, during the height of late seventies punk enthusiasm, featured a twenty-minute version of The Lord's Prayer accompanied by Sid Vicious on the drums. Sioux appeared in a floor-length black-and-white polkadot fur and gigantic feathered Indian mask, which she removed to reveal dramatic make-up. Her long, shaggy, dark mane teased out into a mop, and eyes encircled by great rings of eyeliner and eyeshadow contributed to her dark and spooky image. In 1986 she continued to sing in a piercing soprano, which changed into screams and yodels in the course of lyric themes of death and mayhem. Subjects of her most recent album, *Tinderbox*, range from child molestation ("Candyman"), to murder ("92," statistically, the temperature at which she claims most murders are committed), and apocalypse ("Cities in the Dust"). According to legend, Siouxie and the Banshees see their show as ritual and claim to be in touch with a

*P*atti Smith, early 1980s

sense of ancient mystery rites.

East German-born Nina Hagen still proclaims in 1986, "I'm the mother of punk so what the funk." Posturing in one outrageous costume after another, she has parodied in song and gesture everyone from David Bowie's Ziggy Stardust to Marilyn Monroe and Flash Gordon. When, in 1972, she failed to gain entrance to the government-controlled East German Actor's School, she sang with a Polish band and later graduated with honors from the Studio for Popular Music (Studio für Unterhaltungmusik). By 1973 she also started (and subsequently left) the bands Automobil and Fritzens Dampferband (Fred's Steamboat Band). When her stepfather was expelled from East Germany in 1976, Hagen also went with him and soon after signed a recording contract with CBS Germany. From there it was on to the London punk scene, where she rejoined members of her first band and shaped a chameleon persona with humor, riotous make-up, bits of ratty clothes, and such toys as ray guns. For her 1981 New York debut at the Ritz, she dressed in a turquoise leotard and black leggings, nurse's apron, silver-green hair twirled into dreadlocks, a foot-long black dildo attached to her rear with looping belts and hooks, and short motorcycle boots. Although American radio has not been enthralled by her recorded reinterpretation of the Tubes' "White Punks on Dope," she has built a reputation in Europe as a punk superstar. In 1985 her album *Nina Hagen in Ekstasy* continued the stance of aggressive defiance with savage remakes of "The Lord's Prayer" and

*S*iouxie *fronting the Banshees, 1986*

Sinatra's "My Way." If Siouxie is the dark goddess of the underworld, Hagen is her blonde harlequin foil, the trickster who mocks convention.

*A*dam Ant, 1983

NEW WAVE

New Wave was simply a music-industry repackaging term for musicians who had absorbed elements of the punk stance but omitted its gleeful terror and nasty S&M image. These groups had no unifying musical sound, but they looked nicer, tended to dress either in avant-garde fashion or at least had a

*A*nnie Lennox, ca. 1984

*N*ina Hagen, 1982

definite sense of visual style. In 1978–79 Elvis Costello (né Declan McManus) appeared as a Buddy Holly look-alike while singing "sometimes I think that love is just like a tumor./You've got to cut it out" (from "Lipstick Vogue"), and "I don't want to be a lover./I just want to be your victim" ("The Beat").

In 1980 Malcolm McLaren and Vivienne Westwood dressed up Adam Ant (né Stuart Goddard) and, later, the Bow Wow Wows in pirate garb, thereby launching both the musicians as well as the fashion of the waistcoated New Romantics. The pirate look was one of McLaren and Westwood's most successful clothing themes and changed the boutique image overnight. McLaren reported to *Woman's*

Wear Daily (March 26, 1985) how he came up with the idea: "In London at that time, people were taping off the radios instead of buying records. I was in the process of thinking about Adam, what to do for the band, when it hit me, these people were modern pirates, stealing from their own culture. I thought the concept of pirates was perfect for clothes . . . sun, seas, Errol Flynn, anti-punk rock, gold against black, brass against silver and brocade." Although the pirate-bandit-cowboy archetype has definite mythic origins, the image loses its masculine power if it is too highly decorative. In 1981 Adam Ant wore different costumes, hairstyles, and make-up for each song he performed on video: from swashbuck-

*B*oy George, 1985

ling bandit for "Stand and Deliver" to a fairytale regent in "Prince Charming." Other British bands, like Visage, the Teardrop Explodes, and the Psychedelic Furs, adopted a vaguely New Romantics image, but the look was too fashionable to be perceived as a rebel stance.

THE NEW ANDROGYNE

From 1980 to 1983, Annie Lennox of the Eurythmics and Boy George (né George O'Dowd) of the Culture Club resurrected the androgyne archetype of the previous decade and reintepreted it through fashion. Although Lennox has changed her costume continually, she became famous at first by wearing

pin-striped tailored men's suits and short-cropped, spikey punk-styled orange hair. By 1985 she was fashionable, or perhaps fashion had caught up to her. She appeared in a gold lamé suit and platform shoes, big shirts, and baggy trousers covered in Hebrew lettering, which Sue Clowes had designed for Boy George. By 1986 she had performed in music television videos in a range of outfits, from a fantasy medieval gown and long blonde wig for "You Must Be an Angel," to neat, close-cropped hair and nude shoulders in "Baby's Comin' Home."

Boy George revived David Bowie's wearing of skirts from the early seventies, but most teens were too young to remember it and found the image just the ticket to bother their parents with. George was also terrific for the British fashion industry.

Born in 1961 in South London, he was inspired as a teen by gaudily dressed glam rockers like Bowie. At first he merely dyed his hair orange and wore platform shoes, but, inspired by the 1976 no-holds-barred punk costume party atmosphere, he came into his own. His hair was mauve and he used to go out with a green face, or a blue face and red neck, then a Teddy Boy-vintage outfit, and was finally a success on the club scene when he dressed up in a nun's habit. By the time he started singing in 1981, he was already one of the most infamous of London's demimonde.

Fashion designer Sue Clowes made George's first smocks, which were printed with crosses and airplanes (meant to signify "the destruction of purity") and also those with Hebrew lettering, which he wore with a black Hasidic hat and braided ersatz dreadlocks. In 1984 George wore Vivienne Westwood's World's End shoes, Bay City Roller-styled tartan trousers, blue and silver kimono, and silver straw hat. He held his silver star-shaped guitar in hands adorned with black wet-look gloves, rhinestone-jeweled rings *over* the gloves (reminiscent of Alvin Stardust, 1974). Alternative outfits included his long, oversized stars-and-stripes dressing coat and red-and-blue top hat with ruffled crown. Designer Dexter Wong made most of his outfits in this period, although Wendy Dagworthy made the dollar-sign jacket, and Katherine Hamnet produced the track suits with such slogans as SAVE THE WORLD and CHOOSE LIFE. His kilt was by ModyMap.

Boy George authored a heavily illustrated book featuring his costumes, with patterns and make-up instructions for every Boy George wannabe. Many of his fans who dressed up in his outfits were females. By 1986 he was in pants and short hair, with subdued make-up and elegant coats that were less costume and more mainstream fashion.

Both Annie Lennox and Boy George were transitional figures between chic shock and the more polished musical style of syntho-pop of the mid eighties. Their music was also very professionally produced and appealed to a wide popular audience. However, Sigue Sigue (pronounced "Zig, Zig") Sputnik represents the logical conclusion of image-consciousness and the cult of personality without any signature identity as musicians with a distinct sound.

Bassist leader and former clothing designer Tony James picked guys for the band who had never played any instrument because looks, not musical ability, was his criterion. He claimed "It's much easier to teach someone to play the drums than to teach them to be thin." Now clad in shocking-pink, red, and black skin-tight leathers with fringe, thigh-high stiletto boots, Tina Turner-type wigs also dyed red, white, pink, and black, with white face and black eye make-up, they look like hybrids of several archetypes together (cartoon punk/cowboy/Indian/androgyne). They sold t-shirts with their name on them before they had even cut a single record. Although the British press had derided them as "the biggest rip-off since the Sex Pistols," their first single, "Love Missile F1-11," flew to number three on the British pop music charts in only two weeks.

*M*artin Degville of Sigue Sigue Sputnik, 1986

James describes its sound as like "Elvis Presley crashing the space shuttle against the wall" and considers it primarily a soundtrack for their video, "Immaculate Conception," which is a promotion piece for a projected film and not a mere record for listening to. Everyone who works for Sigue Sigue Sputnik has to promote their look, and James hired an all-girl crew he dubbed the Ultra Vixens and dressed them in rubber miniskirts, high stiletto heels, and Barbie-doll wigs (claiming that even if the women can't move their equipment themselves in these constricting outfits, their looks attract plenty of men willing to help out). His plans for the group include films, television, fashion, publishing, and "maybe even a leisure park." In addition, "we promote sex, violence, glamour, fantasy, and success," says James.

Trans-Atlantic rock critics who so enthusiastically promoted punk as class rebellion, earthy musical back-to-basics, and rejuvenating high-velocity performance energy obviously did not foresee the conclusions of both the style and politics of punk as applied by practitioners of advanced capitalism. With the right video director, clothes, make-up, and hairstyle, the sound of rock took a back seat not only to the look but also to marketing spin-offs in every other media.

Disco to Syntho-Pop

A SOUND IN SEARCH OF AN IMAGE

The sound began almost imperceptibly, grew until it consumed the entire popular music industry, and nearly expired before it attached itself to archetypal images that audiences could recognize as part of their own past. The electronic sound capable of adapting to any and every type of music never actually died. It continued to mix with every genre, from reggae to white electric dance music and the work of mainstream pop artists of the 1980s.

The anti-disco hostility at the end of the 1970s seems to have resulted from displacement of the human presence as the transmitter of rock mythology. In his book *Urban Rhythms*, Iain Chambers noted that, since the 1960s, fans have wanted more from popular music than records. They attended live

Donna Summer, ca. 1976

concerts in order to make personal connections with a mythic community and to surrender to a charismatic leader. But heterosexual white males could not identify with black female disco stars, electronic synthesizers, or the gay background of which the music was so much a part. Not until the early eighties did rock find new figures to deliver the space-age sounds in a familiar guise.

Beginning with a few tricks in the recording studios, then moving on to more high-tech audio advances, musicians have found an ingenious use for every new electronic device. Indeed, electronically processed sounds have been essential to popular recorded music since the late forties. In 1948, Les Paul and Mary Ford, a guitar and vocal duo, distributed sound back and forth between separate monoaural tape recorders to achieve desired effects. In the early fifties, Paul created sonorous textures with the multitrack equipment then available. Sam Phillips, owner of Sun Records, enhanced the vocals of both Elvis and Jerry Lee Lewis with deep echoes, and producer Phil Spector became famous in the early sixties for his "wall of sound," composed of layers of overdubbed sonorities. Brian Wilson, of the Beach Boys, used even more electronic resources than Spector for the 1966 *Pet Sounds* album. It flopped in the U.S.A., but in Britain was recognized as important. However, Wilson's follow-up composition in 1966, "Good Vibrations," which flaunted virtuoso studio production, was a smash hit. Following with electronic collages in their 1967 *Sergeant Pepper's Lonely Hearts Club Band* album, the Beatles officially canonized processed instrumentation. Although Robert Moog invented a commercially available synthesizer in 1964, it wasn't until the early seventies that a portable stage version became widely available to rock musicians. By then a whole aural vocabulary and new way of thinking about popular composition were in place. Multi-track taping had taught rock musicians to treat both instruments and voice as symphonic components of color and texture rather than as solo blocks of sound. By the end of the seventies, elements of the studio techniques had become so democratized that disc jockey rap musicians could assemble complete compositions without learning to play a single traditional instrument—or even a synthesizer.

FINDING THE LOOK OF LOVE

The image-making to suit the new music had to overcome certain sci-fi-sounding musical effects used to excess by synthesizer wizards of the early seventies, who specialized in evoking feelings of cosmic emptiness (some of this output was called "head music"). Science fiction heroes have utopian archetypes dating to Sir Thomas More's *Utopia*, published in 1516, Francis Bacon's 1627 philosophical romance *The New Atlantis*, or the two novels about space travel to other worlds, *Voyage to the Moon* and *History of the Stages and Empire of the Sun*, by soldier-writer Cyrano de Bergerac who lived between 1619 and 1655 (and who was also the hero of a play by Edmund Rostand). However, such artists as Kraftwerk and Giorgio Moroder did not sufficiently romanticize their productions with flamboyant imagery. What is wanted in fantasy is complete distancing not only from the ordinary, but also from over-awareness of virtuoso technique.

The problem of visual representation in highly processed musical performance is similar to what was faced in the early Hollywood musical films, an equally technical and complicated medium. Both rock and the film musical placed a premium on the appearance of freedom, spontaneity, and youthful amateur naturalism, in addition to suggesting a community with the audience. Both aspired to seem like folk art, in which the audience has the potential of becoming a performer. The films tried to break down the psychic distance between singers and audience, inherent and inevitable in reproductive media, through a series of dance and camera techniques and story-telling devices—all of which are used in syntho-pop music videos of the 1980s. The videos, like the films, have tried to make adults appear to be teenagers. Just as Judy Garland was kept in kiddie garb longer than credible for her years, until 1986 twenty-six year old Madonna used progressively more adolescent costume images as she aged. Both media use choreographed group dancing as ersatz spontaneous folk ritual; both feature a backstage fellowship of performers as a means of inviting audience empathy with the team effort; and both switch back and forth between direct address from the proscenium, in costume, and narrative sequences in which the audience eavesdrops on singers in off-stage dress.

In traditional rock, the live stage performance of vaudeville-style hard-sell singers supplied an uninterrupted flow of energy from musicians to audience. But a person sitting at a synthesizer, pushing buttons, hardly projects the passion Jerry Lee Lewis brought to *his* keyboard.

Perhaps the main appeal of disco was that it was the first big revival of dance music in many years. People wanted to dance and dress sexily—women in glossy Spandex leotard tops and hot pants or dance dresses, and men in tight designer jeans and close-fitting tops. The massive American wave started in 1973 in gay clubs with the importation of African Cameroon pop artist Manu Dibango's "Soul Mokossa" (recorded in France in 1972), built to popular saturation by 1976, and continued to the end of the decade. Rock critics have cited the formative influence of black soul hits like James Brown's "Cold Sweat" (1967), "Mother Popcorn" (1969), and "Superbad" (1970); "War" of Motown's Edwin Starr (1970); the Temptations' "Papa Was a Rolling Stone" (1972); Stevie Wonder's singles "Superstition" (1972) and "Living for the City" (1973); and the early seventies sound produced by

Gamble and Huff with seductive songs by Barry White and Isaac Hayes.

Many musicians jumped onto the disco bandwagon in the mid seventies, most of whom left little distinctive musical or visual imprint of their own, letting the fad carry them and dropping out quickly. Thus the style cultivated very few lasting figures who could represent any specific image for fans to identify with. The emphasis on electronically processed sound, its mood of erotic contentment, and its black/Hispanic/gay trappings offered no satisfaction to angry, aggressive, sexually frustrated white adolescents aspiring to resurrect the rockabilly sounds of the fifties and early sixties.

The women who fronted the disco electronics with vocals did do much to humanize the music and enshrine it mythically with their personifications of the Great Goddess. Examples of successful disco divas mark the years of the style: Gloria Gaynor ("Never Can Say Goodbye," 1974), Vicki Sue Robinson ("Turn the Beat Around," 1976), Donna Summer ("Love to Love You Baby," 1976), Diana Ross ("Love Hangover," 1976), Thelma Houston ("Don't Leave Me This Way," 1977), Alicia Bridges ("I Love the Nightlife," 1979), and Blondie ("Heart of Glass," 1979). It was perhaps the first popular music category that allowed women an emphatic entry (not punk's back-door token admittance) into the male musical closed shops. Though it is true that the Italian American *male*, John Travolta (á la Frankie Avalon-Fabian-Bobby Rydell), bleached out and popularized disco for the American suburbs in the 1978 film *Saturday Night Fever*.

As in previous decades, the good-bad polar-

ity of star images persisted. If Donna Summer, the only black disco performer still at the top of the music charts at the end of the seventies, represented the good fantasy princess, Grace Jones, who still produced hits into the eighties, was its dark "Demolition Man" (one of her singles). Ms. Summer's frothy and glorious gowns were the antithesis of the sinister comic-strip jungle animal and robot imagery Grace Jones sported in the late seventies. In 1977 and 1978, Larry LeGaspi made outfits for Jones's theatrical night-club act. In one production number, the stage lights rose on a live caged tiger while music played. The lights dimmed while Jones, clad in LeGaspi's hooded, airbrushed tiger-striped Spandex body suit, metal fingertip claws made by Richard Erker, a horse tail (which she added herself), and carrying a hunk of raw meat, entered the cage. When the lights came up again, the illusion was that the tiger had turned into the singer.

Another memorable creation was a red one-legged, one-shoulder draped gown in which one bugle-beaded cobra bit at Jones's breast while another one wrapped around her exposed leg from ankle to knee (it was held on by elastic dyed to match her skin). The ensemble was topped with a Nefertiti hood with a snake on it. LeGaspi also created a shamanistic hooded cape with red fox tails affixed to beige suede that was cut away in front. The flesh-colored body suit underneath evoked an impression of nudity, save for the dangling fox tails.

Beginning in 1979, fashion photographer and stylist Jean-Paul Goude not only enhanced

*G*race Jones, *dressed by Azzedine Aläia, 1986*

Jones's visual androgyny, but also shifted her image toward that of the science fiction alien by painting her skin blue-black in an attempt to create a unique model of beauty that transcended both gender and race. In 1979–80, she performed in Goude's series of hard geometric forms, which included the cone, flat circle, a rigid bustier molded to her torso, and cylinders encircling her forearms and lower legs. In

*G*race Jones, *1986*

a 1983 interview in *Art and Text* (no. 10), Goude stated that Jones also adopted highly tailored couturier designs because he decided that conventional women's attire made her look male, but masculinely styled outfits enhanced her femininity. She alternated a pants suit and stiletto heels with a massive gorilla costume in her video "One Man Show."

In 1986 she extended her sinister persona to film, in *Vamp*, where she played a vampire strip-tease artist stalking the stage in Kabuki make-up,

flame-red hair, and coiled-wire costume. The androgynous vamp, attractive both to men and women, also falls within ancient legend. Theda Bara, the first androgynous female vamp Hollywood offered as an object of sex fantasy, rose to superstardom within a few months of the release of her first film *A Fool There Was*, in 1915. That film was adapted from a stage play of the same name inspired by Rudyard Kipling's poem "The Vampire," which in turn had been suggested by a Pre-Raphaelite painting of the mythic subject. David Bowie, another androgyne-alien stage character, took on the vampire tradition in the 1983 film *The Hunger*.

The Village People, an all-male group, provided much-needed comic relief in 1979 with their hit disco singles "Macho Man" and "YMCA," in which they parodied gay macho stereotypes with lyrics and costumes ranging from seminude muscle flexers, to leather man, cowboy, and Indian. Either Middle America genuinely appreciated the gay humor or else didn't get what the songs were really all about.

Blondie, disco's white sex goddess, fused the electronic sound with mainstream pop to become one of the first syntho-pop heroines in 1978–79. Her association with New York's CBGB club linked her with such New Wave performers as the Talking Heads and Patti Smith, but costumes by designer Stephen Sprouse shaped her sophisticated "dumb" parody of the bleached-blonde Marilyn Monroe caricature. Whether in t-shirt or sheath dress, she gave the disco sound the needed nostalgic link with the

*M*adonna, ca. 1985, and Cyndi Lauper, ca. 1984

Debbie Harry of Blondie, 1976

as the seductive child-woman in the video "Like a Virgin," she popularized belly-button viewing with cropped shirt tops and exposed bra straps, sixties miniskirt, and lingerie worn as outerwear with lots of thrift-store costume jewelry, hanging crosses, and rosary beads. The image was opportune for teen Madonna wanna-bes, who could ransack attic, basement, and fleamarket for similar accessories. Onstage, during the Virgin tour, she also wore an elaborately embroidered jacket reminiscent of the psychedelic era, which was being revived in fashion during 1984–85. By 1986 she cut her hair short, in an evocation of the innocent Audrey Hepburn look, and romanticized teen pregnancy in her video "Papa, Don't Preach," in which she alternately played a teen unwed mother-to-be in jeans and a gyrating siren singing and dancing in strapless bustier, skin-tight toreador pants, high heels, and formally waved coiffure.

Cyndi Lauper, Madonna's chief rival and polar good-girl antithesis, also plays in vintage mix-and-mismatch costumes. Like Madonna, she used corsets as outerwear, sported a wild tangle of hair, and wore loads of cheap jewelry. Unlike Madonna, and more like Janis Joplin, she has stressed individuality and humor by putting together wacky combinations of separates so as not to appear the sexual stereotype. She works within the harlequin clowning tradition—in which women have participated since the seventeenth-century commedia dell'arte. Past costumes combined with visual associations in a manner that has been described by Cris Crocker, in his book *Cyndi Lauper*, as "either flamenco-dancer-turned-urban-guerrilla or gypsy from outer space."

past that rockers adored, no matter how much they might have hated the idea of disco. When Blondie's group disbanded it was just a matter of time until another female picked up the successful stereotype and gave it one more go-round.

Whereas Blondie played the archetype with tongue in cheek, Madonna acted the bad-girl sex kitten on- and off-stage. Her 1983 video of her hit single, "Material Girl," featured her in fifties-styled coiffure, satin sheath ball gown, and white fur (until the ending, when she exited with a poor boy). Next,

Her hair has metamorphosed through several shades of red to a vibrant cadmium yellow, deep with red streaks, which upon occasion may be wrapped in bright gauzy scarves, while her eye make-up has at different times included day-glo color patches, polkadots, stripes, or flower graphics on her eyelids.

In 1986 she diffused her 1960s gypsy thrift-shop harlequin into an image with such diverse associations that it threatened to diminish the previous instantaneous impact of her persona. Whereas Madonna went through quick image changes one at a time, Lauper's repertoire of outfits on her *True Colors* album cover contains a dominant bohemian outfit, two glitter glamour outfits in mirrored frames, and back-cover nude head-and-shoulder shot with traditionally applied glamour-queen make-up. The dominant costume, made of a newspaper-strip circular skirt revealing the tops of her pull-up, off-white stockings, is paired with a blue chambray paint-spattered blouse trimmed with lace-edged ruffles, both on the three-quarter sleeves and collar, and a pair of painted gold-and-silver shoes. It suggests the role she has already proclaimed verbally in calling herself a "multi-media artist." Blue lipstick, white underbrow eye make-up, contemporary plastic black-and-white bracelet, and artsy earrings also remove nostalgia from the image by placing it within avant-garde fashion. Whether the intimations of East Village painter will be too esoteric for Middle American teens remains to be seen. An alternate 1986 tour costume image is that of a country-and-western barn dancer gone glittery with velveteen bustier and lamé-tiered petticoats that resemble square-dance skirts. These petticoat skirts have been created by New York designer Katy K. Lauper also wears a green-and-peach crinoline petticoat as outerwear with a marbleized bustier to match. Coming years should reveal whether such artistic aspirations will kill the popularity of the rock star.

QUEEN OF THE PACK

If any woman deserves the title of Queen of Rock 'n' Roll, it is Tina Turner a hundred times over. From her first hit singles with her former husband, Ike Turner, between 1960 and 1975, to her triple-platinum (three million sales) album *Private Dancer*, of 1984, and her wide-ranging 1986 album *Break Every Rule*, Ms. Turner has transcended music-industry ghettoization and has survived fad and fashion as well. She has remained the supreme rock goddess with universal popular appeal and a passionately erotic presence unequaled by women half her age. Although most of her youngest fans of the eighties may be more familiar with her work through music videos, her stage act draws an audience of all ages into a vortex of ecstasy. Theater critic John Lahr describes her effect on him in his book, *Astonish Me:*

Everything about Tina's act creates the illusion of mythic gesture. When she backsteps into the chorus line the theatrical effect is thrilling. Who is she? Part animal, part wonder-woman. She swims. She bucks. She swoops her arms in the air like a cowboy cracking a bullwhip. She teases an audience with the innuendo of her voice. She can make them remember their sex; and her body—as sleek and playful as a pony—is also a metaphor which inspires an elaborate reverie. The magic has to be faced, not magnified. On stage she is larger than life. Television shrinks her; films miss the riveting, erotic im-

mediacy of her performance. Even my binoculars are unfair for this kind of spectator sport. The illusion is perfectly calibrated for the naked eye.

In the early sixties, when her song material was gospel-dominated rhythm and blues, Ike Turner renamed Tina (neé Anna Mae Bullock) and dressed her for the stage. According to legend, both the name and costume concept came out of Ike Turner's childhood obsession with such Hollywood jungle adventure films as the Tarzan series and Sheena, Queen of the Jungle, comic books. Tina's skimpy, raggy-looking animal-striped dresses and the long wig hanging down her back followed the Sheena model. Studio press photos were much more demure, with Tina in trim sheath dresses; indeed, for Ike and Tina Turner's 1966 European tour, Azzaro, a fashionable Italian designer, created her outfits. As the psychedelic era emerged, Ike visually updated the act with flower-power paisley and, on occasion, even wore a Beatles-type wig with bangs and, later, an Afro.

After Ike and Tina Turner parted, Tina worked a nightclub act on her own, supplied with outfits as well as moral support by Bob Mackie. "The help I got was from people who liked Tina Turner the person," she said in an interview (quoted in *Tina* by Bart Mills), "not those who liked Tina Turner the star. One big boost I remember was from Bob Mackie. He's the best costume designer for entertainers in Hollywood. He was a big help in showing me how to dress professionally." But when she

Tina Turner, 1985, and dressed by Bob Mackie in "angel wing" costume, 1981

abandoned the club format to do hard rock, she adopted the current rocker uniform of skimpy shirt top and leather miniskirt or tight pants with a broad-shouldered leather or denim jacket. By the time of her 1984 sweep back into mass fame, she sometimes

Tina Turner, 1973

wore Azzedine Aläia's skin-tight futuristic couture.

This science fiction archetype was also reinforced by her 1985 film appearance in *Mad Max Beyond Thunderdome*, in which she wore a metallic mesh clinging dress, with ragged tail hem between her legs, layered, triple-tier projecting shoulder shapes, and mesh gauntlets designed by Norma Moriceaux. But the outfit also evoked her early jungle queen phase, with African-looking multiple-hoop earrings and headband binding her savage mop of hair. That same year she projected an equally tough image at a Live Aid concert to benefit hunger in Africa when she sang a duet with Mick Jagger, in a heavy-metal black-leather mini-skirted outfit topped by a leather bustier with heavy shoulder straps that laced up the front and that were decorated by a strand of metallic tubing. Her accessories included dangling silver earrings, which looked like keyrings loaded with keys, black fish-net stockings, the highest black stiletto heels possible, and blazing scarlet lipstick.

By contrast, the photo cover of her 1986 album *Break Every Rule* signaled a shift to a less hard-edged image with a softer, longer, and fuller shaggy strawberry blonde hairstyle, more naturalistic make-up with less prominent lipstick, a single strand of pearls around her neck, and a strapless matte-black sheath dress slit high on the thigh, partially covered by a soft, black kid-glove leather blouson jacket.

Recalling the Cher of the 1970s, Tina Turner's fine high-cheekboned face has something cross-cultural about it. Combined with a straight-hair, light brown wig, it can look multiracial—a bit American Indian, black, white, Hispanic, and even a little Oriental mixed in. But whereas Cher seemed unable to compete with the power of her face and costumes, Turner's strong stage persona takes charge of any outfit. The clothes don't wear *her*. Likewise, the power of her vocal delivery gives syntho-pop guts, excitement, romance, and body

heat. Although bad-girl/bad-boy archetypes often generate more press coverage because of public and critical outrage, Tina Turner vindicates the side of the good goddess with record sales. Both in costume and performance, she effectively replaces the aesthetic of outrage with one of ecstasy.

DEMOCRATIZING THE STUDIO SOUND

While white rockers generally seem intent on reviving the look and sound of the past, many young black artists of the late seventies through the mid eighties have pounced on studio advances to make the new sounds speak for contemporary street concerns. Rap records—spoken lyrics over a background beat, and collage of other artists' records, rhymes, catch phrases, and commentary—derive from disc-jockey patter, Bo Diddley, dub-reggae, a cappella, doo-wop, Muhammad Ali, George Clinton, street funk, and prototypes stretching back to folk practices in Nigeria and Gambia. Synthesizer music influences include Kraftwerk, Gary Numan, Thomas Dolby, the Human League, as well as the galactic rumbles, throbs, and explosions of arcade video games. All of these elements came together with the availability of electronic drums, double cassette recorders, and teams of turntables, which made it possible to montage, speed-up, and rap over parts of records, which were in turn rerecorded. n

As a kind of space-age doo-wop, rap has taken its clothing from youthful fashions combining casual sportswear, Reebok shoes and sneakers, and such accessories as gloves or hats, which might distinguish a rap group from others on the street. Both rapping and the accompanying break-dancing style are often competitive male enterprises in which groups challenge and reply to each other. Beginning as a street music, rap became part of the popular record industry in 1979 when Brooklyn's First Fatback recorded "King Tim III," the Sugarhill Gang created "Rapper's Delight," and the Furious Five made "Flash to the Beat." By the mid eighties, the electronic style became known as "hip hop," even when it was only marginally associated with the original Brooklyn genre. Although some rappers have appeared on music television in suits and even tuxedos, most dress much less formally than, say, the singing teens from the heyday of "American Bandstand." Except for the mechanized, robotic gestures in break dancing, which evoke science fiction associations, the casual athletic fashions clothe the sound with a democratic image of ideal community that plays against the potentially dehumanized world evoked by high-tech-sounding music.

The biggest stars in the syntho-pop style have cultivated archetypal images that fall into such traditional romantic rock categories as the good or bad boy/girl, the vamp, the clown, the Great Goddess, or the image of ideal community, all of which appeal to the majority of the popular music audience. Other musicians who have used these processed sounds, such as the Talking Heads and Laurie Anderson, have had hit records, but their dominant artistic images and the cerebral elements of their lyrics and fine-arts orientation tend to locate them in art rock more than in syntho-pop.

But if mass popular success depends on creating instantly recognizable archetypal personas, can artists—as individuals—attain mass applause? Or do they require mythic validation to succeed? This is the issue of the next chapter.

Art Rock

By becoming our foremost romantic rebellious culture heroes at a time when cynically manipulative art marketing has compromised the image of the fine artist, rock stars have finally usurped the mythic mystique and shamanistic prestige that traditionally have been accorded to artists. The avant-garde painter, sculptor, composer, or writer, formerly seen as a species of oracular soothsayer, has fallen in public esteem to the profane level of the professional, the smith. Analogous to denizens of Tin Pan Alley, who turned out highly crafted works on demand, today's artists additionally hire press agents and sell their self-images in product adver-

Devo, 1980

tisements. Perhaps it was inevitable that, after the ethos and criteria for avant-garde art became based on understanding the formal and conceptual rules of modern aesthetics and then selectively breaking them, techniques of creation would eventually become ends in themselves and displace the notion of the ineffable in art.

Defection of young visionary artists from the fine-art establishment, which began in the 1960s, brought to popular music a new kind of composer-performer whose scope of work retained traces of his or her previous literary or fine arts training. The output of such individuals has become known as art rock. Although other pop musicians, such as Cyndi Lauper, have begun calling themselves "multimedia artists," their work remains informed by a narrower scope of art history and culture than the music of the art rockers. Nevertheless, the most popular of both types of rock performer fulfill the romantic hero or antihero roles of good or evil figures. For example, the "good" counterculture poets Bob Dylan and the late-phase Beatles contrasted with the "bad" Jim Morrison of the Doors; the futurist "bad" Devo counters "good" Laurie Anderson; and the "good" art-rock modernist David Byrne of the Talking Heads foils the *provocateur* post-modern Malcolm McLaren.

Although the definition of laudable fine art changes as often as the criteria for "authenticity" in rock music, a few traits of the artist have endured in popular imagination. Who an artist is and what he does are outlined in the myth of Daedalus, the sculptor-inventor-architect who worked in the service of sin as well as for the purpose of freedom. When Minos, the legendary king of Crete, struggled to attain his throne, he prayed to the sea god Poseidon to send a white bull as a sign of his divine right to rule. Although he had vowed to sacrifice the arrival to the god, when he marveled at the majesty of the beast, he substituted another bull on the altar and added the divinely sent animal to his royal herd. Poseidon took revenge while Minos was at sea expanding his empire, by inspiring Minos' queen Pasiphae with lust for the bull. Pasiphae commanded Daedalus to sculpt a life-size wooden cow, hollow inside so that Pasiphae could hide in it and thereby approach the bull. The deception worked, the bull impregnated Pasiphae, who bore a monster with the head and tail of a bull and the body of a man. It was known as the Minotaur. Minos ordered

Daedalus to design an inscrutably complex labyrinth to contain the creature, which thereafter was fed on groups of youths from conquered nations as living tribute to the rule of Crete. When Ariadne, the daughter of Minos, fell in love with Theseus, one of the Athenians destined to be a meal for the Minotaur, she sought the aid of Daedalus in saving the youth. Daedalus gave her a skein of linen thread, which Theseus subsequently unwound as he entered the maze and whose linear route he later followed back to the entrance. Daedalus, the master of illusion and invention whose genius placed him outside political and moral codes—his creations could be used for either good or evil—was also something of a tragic figure. After he fell out of favor with Minos, he fashioned wings for himself and his son Icarus with which to effect an escape from Crete. But Icarus flew too close to the sun; the wax in the wings melted, and he plunged to his death in the sea.

Daedalus was a mortal magician-shaman rather than a god, and the figure of the artist ranks lower in popular esteem than immortals like Dionysus, of divine frenzy, or Hermes, the outlaw trickster. Indeed, the artist rarely inspires mass devotion. Fans merge psychically with the rock star, but simply admire and appreciate the mystery, mastery, innovation, and technique of the artist. They may be moved to emotion at the sublimity of an artwork, but they would hardly attempt to tear the artist limb from limb to obtain souvenirs from his body—as they do popular entertainers. The artist gains respect from a relatively small audience; the rock star commands near-religious devotion from hundreds of thousands. The legend of the isolated self-reflective artist is at odds with the unself-conscious ecstasy of rock 'n' roll, the legend of rock community. A critical outsider, the artist comments on but does not participate in the general scene. It is doubtful that the mythologies of art and rock can ever be completely reconciled.

Youth often defines rock in the same way that the teens on "American Bandstand" did in the late fifties and early sixties: If it has a good beat and you can dance to it, it's rock—even if nobody knows what the lyrics are about. In any medium, including rock, the definition of art must be more diverse and cerebral than this. Most people agree that fine art has an element of mastery and complexity unavailable in the basic three-chord techniques of garage bands, though it is true that primitivism and musical minimalism have also been lauded as avant-garde. Others call for the artwork to embody original vision as well.

THE POETS

But nobody called popular music art until 1963 when Bob Dylan's second album, *The Freewheeling Bob Dylan*, established him as the poet of his generation with such songs as "Blowin' in the Wind," "Masters of War," "A Hard Rain's a-Gonna Fall," and "Don't Think Twice, It's All Right." The faults of rudimentary musicianship and a rough, untrained voice with a nasal twang were overlooked in appreciation of the metaphoric density of his ironic narratives, caustic, highly original lyrics, and the creation of a mythic persona that helped propel him to national stardom with startling speed.

Although Dylan (né Robert Zimmerman) came from a solid middle-class background and had attended college for a time, he adopted the working-class hero costume (blue chambray workshirt, jeans, and short haircut) worn by his folksinger idols. Although he was not an orphan, he claimed to be one in the tradition of great heroes in ancient mythology, and was described as merging the characteristics of Huck Finn and James Dean (orphans both) to create a great American persona. He also fulfilled the myth of the magic child who effortlessly achieves what others take decades to learn and accomplish. Commenting on his personal re-creation into a public image, he told a concert audience on October 31, 1964: "It's Halloween and, uh, I've got my Bob Dylan mask on."

His lyrics spoke of himself as the "mystery tramp," the "juggler," the "clown," the "Napoleon in rags"—all personifications of the shaman, jester, and classical harlequin. Defying music-industry categorization, he became known as an artist who poured out his raw thoughts and visions in a torrent of divine spontaneity, in contrast to the sweet dreams deliberately manufactured by professional pop songwriters. The range of his knowledge of literary, poetic, art, and international popular culture extended far beyond that of most of his audience. For example, his "Eleven Outlined Epitaphs" make reference to François Villon, Bertolt Brecht, Brendan Behan, A. L. Lloyd, Charles Aznavour, Yevgeny Yevtushenko, and Miles Davis among others. Indeed, Robert Zimmerman's self-chosen name paid homage to the Welsh poet Dylan Thomas.

Dylan could have stayed an artist with ac-

claim from high culture, but he chose to become a rock star. His presentation of the new androgynous persona and rock-style music at the Newport Folk Festival in 1965 provoked audience outrage at his apostasy. He had discarded chambray for British mod fashion—a stylishly tapered-to-the-body shirt with huge polkadots—and he sported a longer, fluffy, waved hairstyle and dark glasses. By 1966 his face had also acquired a thinner, more delicate cast and an angelic expression that was unlike his former mask of arrogance. In an appearance that year, he wore a close-fitting navy-blue British blazer with a red-and-navy op-art shirt and pointy high-heeled boots. He didn't call himself a poet because he didn't like the word. "I'm a trapeze artist," he proclaimed. From year to year, Dylan continued to express transformations of persona in dress and lyrics that spoke in mythic terms of spiritual pilgrimage, war, heroic sacrifice, resurrection, and most often the courtship of the king's daughter in his love songs to Sara and his lyric reference to Isis, the ancient Egyptian fertility goddess. The costumes moved through country-and-western wear, vaguely Hasidic garb, to hard-rock t-shirt and leather or denim jackets or dark vest with white shirt.

Dylan became the first rock figure to move successfully through extreme changes of both musical and visual styles. When Elvis Presley metamorphosed from working-class hero to glitter king, the clothes changed but his music stayed basically the same—a mixture of rock 'n' roll and sentimental ballad. Dylan not only traded in his art-folk music

*T*he acoustic Bob Dylan, 1962

*J*im Morrison, 1968

for art rock, he kept changing. His transformations weren't easily accepted by a rock public, who wanted immutable heroes, stereotypical characters of one dimension, instantly recognizable and predictable. Proteus, the Greek deity who changed his form at will, was not a popular rock archetype—at least not until David Bowie's blatantly invented and highly exaggerated Ziggy Stardust promoted the idea of creating stage characters as theater. Now it is acknowledged that heavy media exposure will exhaust both the sound and image quickly, and that repetition of one's own work is the kiss of death for artistic development. Artists and rockers have had to unchain themselves from the tyranny of their created images. By 1966 and 1967, American rockers

The electric Bob Dylan, 1964 or 1965

began to become acutely self-conscious about their total image, sound *and* appearance. But the more concisely they developed an image, the more entrapped they became by audience and industry demands for a standardized product.

Jim Morrison of the Doors, whose lyrics dabbled in Brechtian irony and whose music sounded echoes of Kurt Weill in self-conscious phrasing of allusive metaphor, was the dark antithesis of the "good" Dylan between 1966 and 1971. Rock critic Lester Bangs commented on the Doors' style: "The Stones were dirty but The Doors are *dread*." Trained in the fine-arts tradition of theater and film, Morrison crossed over into popular culture to become a new anti-icon of outrage. Although his stage uniform of black leather trousers, well-tailored leather jacket, white shirt, and American Indian silver concha belt was tough, chic, and sexy, his outstanding good looks probably would have made any outfit sing. (By contrast, other contemporary rock groups that were considered avant-garde, such as the Velvet Underground and Frank Zappa, never became mass idols as Morrison did. Morrison's on- and off-stage escapades such as his arrest for indecent exposure, became mythic as the press devoured each incident.) Hollywood wanted to display his body in their films but rejected producing his artistic film work, and Morrison belatedly protested the beefcake approach to the marketing of his image. Although Simon and Schuster published a book of his poetry, the pressures of being trapped within the total pop creation finally proved too much for the artist, who degenerated into a drunken cartoon character and apparently died under unexplained circumstances in Paris in 1971. His young wife also reputedly died within a year, leaving no real evidence of what actually happened. In any event, the double tale of doom served to raise Morrison further to the ranks of mythic rock martyrs.

BRITISH ART ROCK PIONEERS

By never repeating themselves, never imitating their own hits, filling their albums with nothing but hits, and by using avant-garde techniques for mixing environmental sounds with electronic processing and classical orchestral elements, the Beatles, who had already acquired mythic status, popularized the "rock-as-art" phenomenon. While their 1966 *Revolver* album combined classical, pop, jazz, and rock, *Sergeant Pepper's Lonely Hearts Club Band* of 1967 was a complete conceptual statement. The pop opera story (complete with libretto printed on the album's back cover) told of an "Acid Trip for Everyman," using every studio and orchestral device available, plus such noises as barnyard sounds, combs, and kazoos. Acclaimed by personages as diverse as Leonard Bernstein (then conducting the New York Philharmonic) and a *Paris Review* critic for having wedded popular culture to classical art, rock gained media acceptance as an art form.

Although Phil Spector and Brian Wilson of the Beach Boys had used virtuoso and experimental studio techniques to produce innovative popular rock sounds, they were not applauded as fine artists. Art awareness did not inform the *content* of their lyrics, nor did they cultivate an iconoclastic personal image, even though they were popularly perceived as eccentric geniuses with personal problems. The LSD theme of *Sergeant Pepper* established the Beatles as part of the counterculture critical of establishment values, a role traditionally assumed by artists.

The Beatles also reframed their image to conform with the artist archetype. They discarded the clone suits and began to differentiate the way they combed their hair. John Lennon, a former art-school graduate, now wore wire-rimmed granny glasses, and all began to adopt the current bohemian-style hippie outfits. The *Sergeant Pepper* album cover featured the men in colorfully decorated satin military uniforms from Burman's, a theatrical costumer. London fashion boutiques sold identical items within two months after the release of the album, and the Beatles' own Apple Boutique retailed them during 1967 and 1968. While other British art-rock or progressive groups, such as the Moody Blues and Pink Floyd, continued with contemporary-styled musical experimentation, most others within that mode made classical pastiche or kitsch. The Who's rock opera *Tommy* (1969) broke no experimental ground but was nonetheless accepted into the realm of art—though the rockers did not change their costumes accordingly.

By contrast, when Brian Eno was a member of Roxy Music from 1971 to 1973, he established his rock star status through his synthesizer wizardry and striking androgynous stage persona. Eno stood out visually as much as, if not more than, Brian Ferry, the leader of Roxy Music, with his high-camp glittering lamé, feathers, and elaborate make-up. Pencil-thin, he looked as alien as Bowie in Ziggy Stardust drag. But Eno abandoned the public persona and outfits of the rock star in favor of gaining note as an artist when he found that he could not reconcile the two roles. The rock star, imprisoned by his image, was expected to produce work within an identifiably familiar style; the artist wanted to experiment with tangential directions in sound. Yet

Eno continued to shape rock music throughout the 1970s and 1980s as a record producer who manipulates the studio sounds of others, as a collaborator in composition, and as a recording artist with thirteen solo albums and seven singles, even though he relinquished the stage spotlight to those who chose to bear the mythic burden and costume of rockers. He also became a critically recognized fine-arts video artist whose forty-five audiovisual installations have been internationally exhibited in art galleries and public spaces.

Eno claimed that during his tenure with Roxy Music he adopted a feminine costume persona in reaction to masculine clothing, which, he felt, embodied a rationalistic, goal-oriented approach at odds with his intuitive nature, which he perceived as feminine. At that time he also became aware of the pressures of producing work in expensive recording-studio time slots that forced musicians, in the interest of economy, to focus on tried-and-tested procedures instead of attempting anything really new. He fell back on his Ipswich Art School and Winchester School of Art training to devise methods for resisting the commercial paths of least resistance.

In an interview with Jim Aikin for *Keyboard Magazine* in 1981 Eno said that the teaching faculty at Ipswich determined the course of his work. The school's staff of artistic revolutionaries not only encouraged creative thinking, they spent the first semester breaking down students' preconceptions and ready-made answers. After graduating from the

*R*oxy Music, ca. 1973

Winchester School of Art in 1969, he worked with several local experimental bands before becoming a pop musician in Roxy Music. To counter professional pressures Eno developed what he called "oblique strategies" in the form of aphorisms and instructions on notecards that followed the tradition of Marcel Duchamp's notes from *The Green Box* of 1957 (such as "Take a Larousse dictionary and copy all the so-called abstract words—those with no concrete reference. Compose a schematic sign designating each of these words."), painter Jasper Johns's famous dictum, "Take something and do something to it. Do something else!," or the instructional scores of 1960s avant-garde composers Eno admired, such as John Cage and La Monte Young, which might tell a performer to sit at a piano for a specified length of time and to do nothing, or to repeat a sound sequence over and over. Eno's dicta included: "Emphasize the flaws," "Make an exhaustive list of everything you might do and do the last thing on the list," or "Once the search is in progress, something will be found."

Yet he also stated in the same interview that breaking and making rules was not what good music was about for him, and that he owed a debt to John Cage for introducing him to the notion of spirituality and philosophy within music-making. After an initial foray into what he called (in a 1986 *Artforum* interview) "little pop versions of Duchampian tricks" with several albums of songs, getting a sense of mystery and magic into his work became a goal. His means of achieving this in his solo instrumental compositions was the removal of commonplace pop music tunes, chord patterns, and beats, and an emphasis on sonic textures produced by a synthesizer. The resulting cerebral effect of his sonic textures made his work known as "head music." His process of using disconnected, objectified sound in an abstract way had something in common with the musical achievements of composer Erik Satie (1866–1925), although they differed greatly in acoustic style. Yet Eno's collaboration with pianist Harold Budd, in *The Plateau* (1980), echoed Satie's limpid simplicity of melody, especially in their "Not Yet Remembered," which recalls in its atmosphere of lyric serenity, Satie's "Dream of Pantagruel's Childhood" (1915), and in their title "Chill Air," which echoes Satie's title "Cold Pieces (Three Airs Put to Flight)." Other solo albums by Eno, such as *Discreet Music* (1975) or *Ambient Music for Airports* (1978), took as their theme "ambient music," which Eno conceived of as acoustical landscapes and for which he claimed indebtedness to the minimalist avant-garde styles of composers La Monte Young and Terry Riley.

Eno's alternating work in popular rock 'n' roll included collaboration on three David Bowie albums, production of three more with the Talking Heads, a compositional collaboration with David Byrne, and production of albums for Devo and Ultravox. Eno's personal trademark in these albums often centers about his manipulation of sound with reverberations, echo, and other electronically produced effects to produce a sense of psychoacoustic space in which a location or context is evoked, but not specifically illustrated (the aura of African wilderness in *My Life in the Bush of Ghosts*, composed with David Byrne, is an example). Eno also cites Karlheinz Stockhausen, the Beatles' "I Am the Walrus," and Steve Reich as his predecessors in collaging "found" aural materials into one's work.

The removal of aural narrative from Eno's music paralleled the stripping away of mythic associations in costume. Beginning with the 1973 and 1974 albums of songs with ambiguous lyrics, which he composed and performed himself, the album cover images finally dropped the glam representations of Eno by 1975, as his work became predominantly artistic in its focus. In the tradition of Daedalus, Eno has crafted rock music for performers whose public images are either positive or negative, while he transcends the limitations inherent in either polar type.

THE FUTURISTS

In 1975 the American band Devo marketed itself as a self-contained art and entertainment package. They wrote their own music and designed their costumes, marketing concepts, and films to showcase their songs. The name *Devo* stood for *devolution*, the idea that civilization is regressing through decadent stages of decline. Although the electronic processing of their sound forecast the syntho-pop of the 1980s, their costumes and surreal narrative plots commanded more attention than their music. Devo's first film, *The Truth About D-Evolution* (1976), which won an award at the 1977 Ann Arbor Film Festival, presented their music with a collage of medical-book freak-show images. In 1977, another film, *Jocko Homo*, a mock march set to the sounds of things falling apart, showed members dancing like herky-jerky marionettes as they sang to a group of science students in a surgical amphitheater while body-stockinged human beings writhed on dissecting tables. The costumes for a 1978 "Saturday Night Live" television performance included antiradiation jumpsuits, colored glasses for viewing three-dimensional films or comics, elbow- and kneepads, and hockey helmets. In stage performance Devo was known to have worn upside-down tiered plastic flowerpots, shiny high-waisted pegged pants and matching jackets, and dark boat-neck knit shirts while they played a combination of Moog synthesizer and traditional instruments. The band cited Stanley Kubrick, Federico Fellini, Russ Meyer, and Luis Buñuel as their major influences. After signing with Warner Brothers Records in 1978, Devo continued to make rock videos into the eighties, works that offended many because of their savagery, incipient fascism, and misogyny. Since cynical satire is not widely applauded in rock—even for bad-boy archetypes—Devo never rose above the status of art-cult figures.

Although Laurie Anderson's art rock also satirizes the sinister aspects of omnipotent corporate technology, the former sculptor (master of fine arts from Columbia University and exhibitor at the Holly Solomon art gallery in New York City), executes it with such coy enchantment that the tragedy of death by industrial carelessness, alienation of look-alike housing (where one can walk unknowingly into another's home), or the "city which repeats itself endlessly hoping that something will stick in its mind" all become equally amusing. As *rock*, the act suffers from terminal gentility. As *art*, it is enervated by too many special effects and techniques with electronic

Laurie Anderson, ca. 1984

gadgetry, all of which mask trivial content. But for those who can neither take art nor rock straight, it's superb entertainment and extraordinarily appealing to the college-educated audiences who can appreciate literary and art allusions.

Anderson recasts the avant-garde into minstrelsy using narrative prototypes, the serial minimal music of Philip Glass, and science-fiction imagery from such books as William Burroughs's *Nova Express*, *The Penny Arcade Peep Show*, and *The Wild Boys*. As with conventional rock lyrics, Anderson's songs express poignant nostalgia for the myth of golden days—in her case, the days before corporations strip-mined a pastoral America and terrorists carried bombs on airplanes. As in fine art, her scope of source models is impressive.

Anderson's short, spikey male haircut and tailored man's white suit with tie establish her within the light, "good" hero androgyne archetype. Since the mythic model of the artist is male, the masculine costume enhances popular perception of the seriousness of her aesthetic intent. Moreover, her rolled-up baggy pants, displaying day-glo pink socks and high-top sneaker shoes, offers the necessary iconoclastic detail that indicates individual taste and wit, and that relieves the severity of the tailored look. In her 1986 performance film, *Home of the Brave*, she alternates outfits: first her signature white suit, next the reverse color with a black suit and white satin shirt, and then a jacket over a long, slinky silver lamé backless halter-top dress. But when she removes the jacket from the outfit, she looks like a kid in mommy's dress rather than a sexy rock goddess; for the stance of the act has cultivated a cerebral distance from the body. This aspect was futher emphasized when she performed a contemporary version of black-face minstrelsy in her video "Sharkey's Day," in which she used Chroma-key electronic effects to make her face and body darkly invisible, save for the luminous delineation of her lips, eyes, and gloved hands. When Annie Lennox of the Eurythmics wears masculine suits, her passionate emotional identification with the lyrics contrasts with the visual impression of restraint in tailored outfits. By contrast, Anderson's cool, well-educated distance from her material and highly stylized stage movements desexualize her stage persona as thoroughly as her treatment of William S. Burroughs's imagery removes all eroticism from her lyrics.

Diamanda Galas, although she does not specialize in science-fiction imagery, plays the artistic dark vampire antithesis to the light, wistful Anderson child-androgyne. Performing in ghoulish make-up, long black hair, black gown, and under dramatic lighting, the operatically trained soprano wildly layers speech, arias, shrieks, and whispers over a collage of prerecorded audio tapes. Although few could call it rock, her violently emotional mode of delivery owes something to the realm of rock theatricality and to the vamp archetype also used by rockers.

MODERN VS. POST-MODERN MYTHOLOGIES

David Byrne and Malcolm McLaren—the "good" hero and the "bad" antihero—extend the romance of mythic polarities in art rock. Both have been acclaimed as renaissance men, whose creative talents extend beyond the music they record to other media. Byrne is not only a musician whose popular success with processed electronic sounds would qualify his band as syntho-pop, but an innovative video artist and writer-director of his own 1986 feature film, *True Stories*. Malcolm McLaren, whose history of artistic endeavor (at this writing) is scheduled to be featured in an exhibition curated by Paul Taylor at the New Museum in New York City in the winter of 1987, first achieved notoriety for establishing the punk-rock movement through his management of the Sex Pistols and then became a recording artist in his own right, continuing to challenge both artistic and rock music conventions.

Around 1977 David Byrne and the Talking

Heads played to audiences primarily consisting of downtown New York City artists. Their art cult appeal was a cerebral excitement that has been described by Ken Emerson in the *New York Times Magazine* as "the hyperventilating rush of an anxiety attack." Byrne was—and still is—the visual focus of the band, with a borderline-psychotic stage persona reminiscent of Tony Perkins in *Psycho*. There was something of the shaman in the charismatic intensity of the singer, who delivered dense lyrics containing cryptic questions that were comments, sensible nonsense, and ambiguous images, all the while seeming on the verge of losing control with turkey-neck tics (whose origin he disclosed in a 1981 interview in *Musician, Player and Listener*: the routines of a group of Los Angeles dancers called the Electric Boogaloos), awkward gestures, and a voice approaching a screech. An intellectual aura reminiscent of Buddy Holly attracted audiences who could identify with neither the lyrics nor the imagery of teenage bad-boy rockers.

Next his stage presence became less anxious, and he dropped the register of his singing voice, but he also heightened his visual idiosyncrasy with a huge white suit so oversized that it immediately established him as *outré*. This suit, which was worn in the concert documentary film *Stop Making Sense* (1984), was created during a performance tour of Japan. Byrne discussed stage outfits with fashion designer Jurgen Lehl, who mentioned that the costumes should be a little bit bigger than real life. Byrne, a former art student at the Rhode Island School of Design, decided that he would be a "Mister Mister man, but a little bit big-

ger" and drew a square on his dinner napkin, which (he decided) represented a symbol of the character. He also noted that Japanese stage dress made the head look tiny and that it evoked a preparatory mental set on the part of the actor and a sense of antic-

David Byrne, 1983

ipation from within the audience. Rock fans might also note that the outfit subtly recalls the huge white tuxedo worn by Chuck Berry, and art connoisseurs remember that hugely oversized costumes were used by Futurist art performers before World War I and were further developed by Picasso in outfits for Sergey Diaghilev's 1917 production of the ballet *Parade*, with music by Erik Satie, scenario by Jean Cocteau, and choreography of Leonide Massine.

The imagery of the mad artist echoes that of Balzac's classic paradigm of modern art, "The Unknown Masterpiece," a story whose conceptual influence on art has been thoroughly discussed by Dore Ashton in her 1980 book *A Fable of Modern Art*. In Balzac's tale, a genius painter named Frenhofer plumbed the depths of his psyche while working on his lifetime masterpiece. The resulting modern painting of abstract forms and lines was unintelligible, even to other painters, save for the appearance of one perfectly drawn naturalistic foot at the bottom of the canvas. When Frenhofer's colleagues expressed their dismay at the work, the artist burned his paintings and committed suicide. The legend of the true artist as a prophetic psychotic on a spiritual quest has sanctioned and validated many avant-garde experimental meanderings as well as ridiculous put-ons. Because, historically, the artistic gift was believed to have been bestowed upon select persons born under specific astrological conditions (see Wittkower's 1963 book *Born Under Saturn*), a psychic predisposition rather than acquisition of techniques and appropriation of images was seen as the definitive trait of artistic genius. This collective mythology also implies that the authentic artist receives original images from the mysterious unconscious, even though he or she may have learned the craft of the medium by studying the old masters. In short, the modernist myth is one of creative virgin birth.

Although more oblique and less personally caustic in social criticism, Byrne's early lyrics of irony as well as more recent 1986 work, which owes a debt to a popular rock style informed by Tex-Mex, southern styles, and country-and-western music, recalls Dylan in mood and even specifically alludes to the older artist (for example, Byrne's 1986 "Dream Operator" refers to Dylan's "Napoleon in Rags" character). Byrne's lyrics, like those of Bob Dylan, seem to pursue a pilgrimage, as for example, "Searchin' for a City to Live In," which reconstructs bits of a black evangelist's exhortations and alludes to Third World folk music. Byrne also stated in a 1981 interview in *Musician, Player and Listener* that his songs from the album *Remain in Light* "have an implied religious spiritual feeling. *Implied* but not stated. I wanted to get a spiritual ambience in the words" and "Almost all the vocals we put on it have to do with one kind of religious experience or another." Byrne also credited African novelist Amos Tutuolo's *My Life in the Bush of Ghosts* as inspiration for the album of that title. Byrne's Parsifalian quest echoes that of such twentieth-century artists as Picasso, Brancusi, and others who explored African and Oriental sources for the power of their atavistic images as well as for formal innovation. That Byrne and Eno appropriated what they termed "found" aural materials was secondary both to the scope and sonic layering that molded their interpretations, as well as to their professed goals of transcendence and their "born under Saturn" artistic personas.

David Byrne directed, starred in, wrote the

music, and conceptualized the scenario for his 1986 feature film *True Stories*. The work further extended the range of his artistic credits, even while it shifted his rock image from that of a freaky New York artist toward something of an eccentric Everyman. His Texas outfits were not only out of synch with what everyone else in the story was wearing, they were also worn with inescapable awkwardness. His western suits were stiff-looking and peculiar, and even his yellow cowboy shirt with black piping trim sagged at the breast pockets, which gaped open. At one point Byrne commented about the strangeness of these costumes, saying: "I can't get used to these outfits. They're selling them in the stores, but I don't see anyone else wearing them." The image was the high school nerd (seen decades later), who wanted to fit in with everybody else but still couldn't.

Malcolm McLaren has played the mythic bad boy in the rock and fashion world for over ten years, but only since 1982 has he crossed over into making art rock under his own name. As the one-time conceptualizer for the New York Dolls, the Sex Pistols, and Bow Wow Wow, McLaren has been excoriated from many sides for appropriating music, images, and ideas from others—a fact he doesn't deny. Perhaps what irritates both the rock and art critics is that he makes undeniably clear the link between fashion and rock (which is anathema to rockers) and, like other post-modern artists, lays waste the modernist myth of virgin-birth art creation, and professes no spiritual aspirations. Indeed, many of his statements to the press focus on profane commerce, the marketing of his products.

Around 1972, the former fine-art student collaborated with clothier Vivienne Westwood on punkish fashion designs, which began with pornographic t-shirts and continued with a series of deliberately provocative styles. These were sold in the couple's clothing boutique in London's King's Road. The store changed names as fast as the owners changed garment styles. After seeing the New York Dolls on a British tour in 1975, McLaren attempted to reshape their image from campy transvestites to that of Communists in red leather suits performing on a stage draped with Soviet flags. When *Rolling Stone* magazine (October 20, 1977) asked McLaren why he presented the Dolls in this fashion, he replied that it was an attempt to find a means of audience provocation that would make the band more extreme and less accessible. "Rock and roll is not just music. You're selling an attitude too."

In 1976, McLaren, Westwood, and situationist artist Jamie Reid designed the Sex Pistols, drawing their raw material from various boutique hangers-on. Although the press mythologized key band members Johnny Rotten and Sid Vicious as emblems of class revolt, their rudimentary music became the *background* sound to punk as fashion, a phenomenon that swept the Western world. Although costume has been inseparable from rock music since the 1950s, it became the paramount feature, thanks to the collaboration of these three visual artists.

According to Iain Chambers in *Urban Rhythms*, the intellectual rationale for their aesthetic of outrage was Reid and McLaren's involvement with the Situationist International move-

*M*alcolm McLaren: Duck in the Oyster *video, 1982*

ment, pioneered by French leftist Guy Debord, who wrote a critique of capitalism entitled *The Society of the Spectacle* in 1970. Between 1952 and 1972, the Situationist organization planned and carried out provocative projects within the Dada tradition, which were designed to turn art into life and life into art to the end of overthrowing the boredom and other alienating aspects of capitalism and society. Jamie Reid, McLaren's friend from Croydon Art School days, has been credited with the politicalization of

the imagery associated with McLaren's rock groups, although Chambers reported that McLaren himself had links with Situationists called the "King Mob," who distributed "free" goods to Christmas shoppers at Harrods Department store—until they were stopped by the police.

Early in 1976, McLaren asked Reid to be the art director of the Sex Pistols, and the artist designed every record sleeve, poster, and handbill until the group disbanded in 1978. Reid has also been credited with writing the song "Anarchy in the U.K." His most infamous graphic image is a transformation of Cecil Beaton's portrait photograph of Queen Elizabeth, to which he added swastikas on the eyeballs and a safety pin through her lip. Reid continued to work with McLaren and Westwood on their 1980 film *The Great Rock 'n' Roll Swindle* and on their next project, the band Bow Wow Wow. His graphic works from the punk era were featured in exhibits in London at the Hamilton Gallery in the spring of 1986 and in New York at the Josh Baer Gallery in the fall of that year.

Like David Byrne, McLaren devised a documentarylike film, hired a scriptwriter to realize his story, and starred in it himself. Unlike David Byrne, he did not direct it; he attempted to mythologize his own experiences with the Sex Pistols, was reportedly disappointed with the results, and was sued by the remaining Pistols over rights to their musical materials. He lost.

In 1980 McLaren and Westwood created the pirate look for Adam and the Ants, but parted from them to form a band that McLaren could shape from scratch. The teenagers he recruited for Bow Wow Wow, fronted by the fifteen-year-old Annabella Lwin, whom he claimed he had met in a laundromat, also sold Westwood's pirate fashion collection during actual performance. McLaren stated in the March 25, 1985 issue of *Woman's Wear Daily* that "it was the most successful concept for clothes we ever did, because it crossed every barrier." And the music? McLaren's lyrics for "W.O.R.K." were somewhat too political for the mass rock audience, and Annabella's recorded delivery lacked great enthusi-

asm, but the group had a 1981 hit in England with "See Jungle, See Jungle," and their stage performance was reportedly popular.

By 1982 McLaren dropped Bow Wow Wow and wrote and coproduced the album *Duck Rock* under his own name, appropriating sounds from existing sources, which he credited in the album liner notes. Westwood produced an accompanying fashion

*M*cLaren and Westwood: Queen Elizabeth with safety pin through the lip, 1976

collection called "Buffalo Gals," with sheepskin vests and wool frock coats, which were supposed to suggest a rural, preindustrial society.

Although David Byrne and Brian Eno had freely adapted and collaged music from "found" Third World folk sources—such as the voice of an

Arabian singer—and a black preacher's rap in the 1981 album *My Life in the Bush of Ghosts*, and they also carefully credited their sources and the musicians in a press release written by Byrne, McLaren's transformations of similar sources in *Duck Rock* were not as readily apparent. Nor was it as clear what he actually wrote himself. Eno and Byrne had

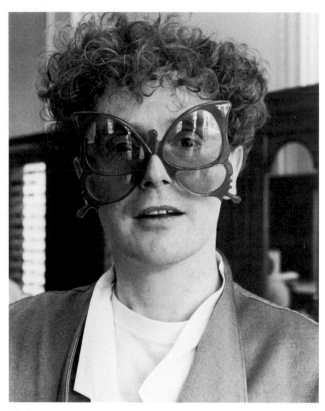

Malcolm McLaren promoting Madame Butterfly *album, 1985*

heavily processed the sounds using a synthesizer, while McLaren had processed his material as dub-reggae disc jockeys had done since 1965 by collaging multiple record sources, as well as scratching the record with sharp objects to obtain a scratching sound. This latter procedure, used in rap since 1979, was not considered a fine-art technique. Eno

and Byrne had each established the mythological persona of fine artist. McLaren, in contrast, created a reputation as a Machiavellian trickster. *Duck Rock* was clearly danceable, and the lyrics had a sense of humor accessible to a mass public—despite multiple cultural references collaged together, as in much contemporary art. The apparent dumbness of such lyrics as "Double Dutch" and the convincing evocation of a call-in radio rap show embraced aspects of popular culture so thoroughly that one was made unsure about whether this was parody, pastiche, art, or put-on.

The fact that it was assembled by a worldly-wise anarchist, rather than an ignorant but talented teen, finally separated the persona of the artist from the apparent content of the songs. Nevertheless, the album was played on black radio stations and could be found in the "Soul" section of many record stores. All that was missing to make him a rock star was personal presence, either onstage or in video performance. The audience had no figure with whom to empathize.

A cynical stance savaged both classical opera and popular music fans in McLaren's next album *Fans* (1984), despite his avowal of innocent intent stated in a *Woman's Wear Daily* interview (March 26, 1985): "I wanted to make an album of love songs, but I couldn't write, 'baby please don't go . . .'" At the same time he claimed that he used operatic voices because they "were filled with passion and a certain naivete that hadn't been squashed by the packaging and production machinery of rock 'n' roll." McLaren himself squashed the operatic material in the production of his rock album, in which he delivered as monologue the story of Puccini's *Madame Butterfly,* a parody of the original delivered in an ersatz midwestern American accent, which associated both the operatic role and Americans with callous stupidity. Misogyny was the underlying attitude in his take-off on *Turandot,* sung by Angie B., whose vocal rendition and phrasing emphasized McLaren's caricature in lyrics about a young, uneducated female rock music fan who took hours to write pathetic fan letters to her performing hero. His posture of condescension to both rock culture and high culture was either art or self-destruction, for by playing the comic who laughs *at* his fans instead of *with* them, he had separated himself in identity from both audiences. Again there was neither costume image nor a stage persona to accompany the album, although McLaren told *WWD* that he had designed a line of clothes associated with the album, but that it had not gone into production. He also said that a stage version was in the offing; it has yet to materialize.

Swamp Thing, the following album (1985), which consisted of outtakes from *Duck Rock,* revealed little other than formula technique and thematic scope reduced to straight pop. Although appropriation of images and sounds has been a venerable modern and post-modern art strategy, the criteria for evaluating artistic results have to do with how well those results explicate or illuminate aspects of its sources in relation to contemporary culture, history, or even its own creation. *Swamp Thing* neither accomplished this nor supplied the mythic visuals or shamanistic persona common to either hard rock or art. But as syntho-pop, the product had a good beat, and you could dance to it.

The success and failure of McLaren reveal that rock music, fine art, and fashion all trade in mythologies that can overlap and reinforce each other. The archetypal rocker is part of and speaks for Everyman/woman. In representing the confrontational and prophetic aspects of perception, the mythic artist stands apart from the popular culture he expresses. Fashion designers refocus and refine rock and art images into precisely marketable products, reinforcing the original sources by echoing them much as the chorus does in a call-and-response gospel song. McLaren's situationalist art rock worked best in collaboration with other artists, when it confronted both popular and high culture. It functioned least successfully without their contributions. As the coordinator of others' talents, and as a salesman of Westwood's designs, his role might be compared to that of today's media-celebrity art gallery directors. McLaren represents both the Mary Boone of art rock and the forebear of the young 1980s post-modernist gallery artists, who publicly proclaim their techniques of market manipulation and divest contemporary art of any mythic or spiritual content through emphasis on the strategies of its production and distribution.

Fashion and Rock Costume

Fashion and Rock Costume

I think that rock stuff is just sexy and that gets narrowed down to women looking like women and guys looking like guys.

Betsey Johnson, fashion and rock-costume designer

*T*he hard-rock image that knows no separation between day and night is sexy and mythic, trashy and democratic; it is high impact, with hot colors and strong contrasts of dark and light. Most Anglo-American sportswear, from preppy to post-punk, trades in virginal androgyny and fictions of newness, elegance, and elitism, with understatement in cool neutrals and a touch of color for accent. But elements of

Betsey Johnson designs, 1986

rock imagery constantly punctuate couture, saving it from the boredom of terminal gentility. When the cover model on American *Vogue* (September 1986), in messy but modified long rock shag hairstyle, poses in one of Geoffrey Beene's lace and sequin strapless gowns, rock is safely sequestered within the separate fantasy realm of evening wear. When Beene, Jean Muir, Yves St. Laurent, and Sonia Rykiel use simulated leopard-spot prints for dresses, which evoke (though look nothing like) Tina Turner's animal raggy creations, they fabricate them not in polyester and acetate but in silk faille and satin. While the values of taste, polish, charm, and elegance make high fashion aristocratic, culture also reinforces the Hollywood costume and vaudeville view of glamorous living, a theme ex-

*C*her, *dressed by Azzedine Aläia, 1985*

ploited by pop or night-club singers like Cher and Diana Ross, who wear fashion designer gowns for performance.

Until Calvin Klein brought us soft-core advertisements for underwear, jeans, and perfume, men and women in contemporary daytime dress tended to camouflage their bodies with variations in tailoring, enveloping knits, or unisex athletic garb. Fashion did not speak of love, it knew neither adul-

tery nor affairs, not even flirtation, Roland Barthes observed in *The Fashion System.* Couture was high culture opposed to the low or pop realm, even when couture appropriated designs from the streets. What changed in the 1980s was that popular performers not only became good-girl/good-boy heroes through their participation in worldwide philanthropic projects, but artists as well. Granted that the majority of rockers still present ignorant and misogynist-narcissist types, but musical stars who have captured headlines with their positive achievements have finally made rock okay for the upper middle class.

Yet designer sportswear fashion still remains distinct from both designer rock costume as well as the antifashion hard-rock stance of *non*-designer jeans, t-shirts, and biker jackets evoking the fifties. Unlike rock costume, fashion lacks such obvious myths—although it does contain certain mythic parables. It postulates a visionary newness, which is distinctive and elitist, even when the styles trade in nostalgia or court the mass market. As such, it is akin to science-fiction romance, which creates a fantasy world of the future while longing for an imagined simple goodness of the past. Roland Barthes also noted the utopian literary quality of fashion, calling it a "formless novel," a narrative founded on the "terminology of a utopian reality" and using themes of nature, exotic geography, history, and art to compose social models presenting an ideal of culture. Fashion is akin to fiction, most specifically science fiction.

In "The Virginity of Astronauts: Sex and the Science Fiction Film," Vivian Sobchack (in the

1985 anthology of essays *Shadows of the Magic Lamp: Fantasy and Science Fiction in Film*) notes that, throughout the genre, female biological traits are usually covered up in unisex garb, except when the women are represented as aliens, in which case they are sexily and scantily clad. Both Sobchack and coauthors Robert Scholes and Eric Rabkin (in their 1978 book *Science Fiction: History, Science, Vision*) believe that science fiction about aliens is an extended metaphor for relations between the sexes. In contemporary male-dominated culture, women are alien, possessing the different body of the "other," which threatens men's autonomy because of its potent ability to seduce and to induce dependency through its association with Mother. Males, like Buck Rogers or even Superman, have a cleancut, muscular sameness—"not homosexual, but homotextual," claims Sobchack, citing Pauline Kael's negative review of the science fiction film *Marooned* (collected in Kael's 1974 *Deeper into Movies*), which inquired, "Who in his right mind could cast the three leads with Gregory Peck, Richard Crenna, and David Janssen, when anybody can see they're the same man?" In contrast, sexy women in science fiction films are usually the evil alien.

One need look no further than John Molloy's best-selling dressing guides, one volume for men and one for women, to see how this notion translates into professional dress. In his section of *The Woman's Dress for Success Book* entitled "Bedroom or Boardroom—Your Choice," Molloy counsels: "Unfortunately, our testing proves that dressing to succeed in business and dressing to be sexually attractive are almost mutually exclusive. Except for very rare situations, you can't do both at the same time. Most men don't try, and those who do try fail, at least in business." Sportswear has also flirted with science fiction and androgynous imagery for decades. Obvious spacesuit metaphors abound in skiwear, two-piece rain ensembles, aviator jumpsuits, hoods, the Courrèges, Pierre Cardin, and Yves St. Laurent sportswear of the sixties, Larry LeGaspi's trapunto-shouldered fantasies for day and evening in the seventies, and the eighties designs of Claude Montana and Thierry Mugler, to name a few. Androgyny returns each decade in different variations: the twenties flat-chested flapper with bobbed hair and without waistline, thirties tailored ensembles even for tennis, hunting, and golf, forties utilitarian wartime outfits, fifties chemise and oversize men's white shirts for teens, sixties unisex denims and army clothes, and seventies and eighties androgynous casuals and unisex athletic garb.

Androgyny in fashionable sportswear often masculinizes or makes women sexless in oversized outfits, while androgyny in rock costume favors the feminization of men. The latter is a transgressive act because it visually transforms males into the alien "other." While Annie Lennox in her pin-striped suits is fashionable, David Bowie or Boy George in skirts is perceived as a sexually aggressive gay drag queen or an alien freak. The masculinization of women's fashion represents a step up the social power scale, while the feminization of male rock garb is a rejection of the establishment class hierarchy.

Like much science fiction, sportswear fash-

ion, as opposed to hard-rock imagery, promotes the modern over the old and the cultured over untamed nature (that is, sex). Peter Biskind's essay "Pod, Blobs, and Ideology in the American Film of the Fifties" documents how natural elements, such as ants, grasshoppers, killer bees, and so on, are depicted as evil, anarchic in a society benefiting from better-living-through-technology. Mass-produced fashion has been a triumph of technology. But while designer-label sportswear most often aspires to cultured upper-class imagery, anonymously crafted lower-class rock dressing deliberately aims to be barbarous. An advertisement for a rock clothing store would never indulge in such rhetoric as this 1986 ad for Perry Ellis designs retailed at Saks Fifth Avenue: "Striking a balance of grace, grandeur, and intimating design to come in the season ahead." Music television and photographs of rock performers are all the advertisement necessary. Erotic vitality is the most important character of rock imagery, whereas sportswear fashion stresses virginal youth, masculinized androgyny, and periodic renewal. This is not to say that rock does not promote youthfulness as a quality, but it is sexual vitality that is foremost in importance. Rock stars can be over forty years old, but they can't look tired or impotent. The mythic magical children of rock music who became stars, such as Brenda Lee, the early sixties British rockers, and even the Beatles costumed to suggest moppets, were perceived as sex objects. Indeed, outside of rock culture, perception of children as sexual beings is regarded as transgressive. In the

Larry LeGaspi, science-fiction trapunto design

late 1970s, when Calvin Klein suggestively posed voluptuous teen model Brooke Shields in his designer blue jeans, and seminude nymphets appeared in high-fashion magazines, public controversy arose and letters of reader protest appeared in to-the-editor columns. By contrast, the prepubescent miniskirt dress styles of the 1960s on such anorexic-looking models as Twiggy were applauded.

If rock and fashion relate differently to social and sexual themes that can be illustrated by the example of science fiction, they also differ in how they relate to more narrowly defined *mythic* themes present in science fiction. The two most common science-fiction mythic motifs analogous to aspects of fashion are the ritual killing of the king and the prolongation of youth. The two themes are closely related: the old king is killed in order to institute the rule of the newborn child. For example, on New Year's Eve, old Father Time gives way to the New Year's baby. Fashion replaces last year's models with much the same ritual regularity as mythology replaces its worn-out deities. The metaphor of eternal youth through renewal of clothes is a variation on the science-fiction theme of creating life from nonliving material. Most fashion models are finished during their mid or late twenties, except for a few who remain as elegant matron types in haute couture. In the world of rock, however, one no longer has to be an adolescent to be a star. The Grateful Dead, Tina Turner, Diana Ross, and other top performers of the sixties have continued to sing to overflow crowds well into the 1980s.

Designer labels move fashion even further from rock mythology and rather closer to the realms of art and of commerce. Labeled as the creation of one person, clothing is no longer anonymous and no longer belongs to everyone. It becomes a signature creation that is—supposedly—the product of a single mind. If this product is something like an art object, it is also very much a *product*. Because of the relatively limited production and higher prices of name designer wear, such garments tend to be associated with elitism and yuppie consumerism. It is this aspect of fashion that many rockers have reacted against. For example, hard rockers like Joan Jett and Bruce Springsteen have consistently resisted the fashion and designer look. It is true that more pop-oriented entertainers have adopted designer fashion, changing their look constantly in order to prevent media exhaustion of their image. However, even these performers usually commission more individualized versions of designer fashion. To buy retail would be to compromise the uniqueness of the persona within its mythic type. Betsey Johnson, who is currently designing the Bangles' new look, explained that the group image has to be exclusive: "I don't think that they can risk wearing something that's in Bloomingdale's. But they want that cut, and they want that feel. . . . But within that they each must have their own personalities."

HISTORIC PRECEDENTS

In the 1950s, rock music belonged to teenagers, even if it wasn't always performed by them, but teens tried to look like adults. Teen fashion was influenced less by the outfits of the rock performers than by the dress of the fans who were televised in the U.S. each weekday on "American Bandstand"

and in Britain on "Ready, Set, Go." "Bandstand" had a dress code that prohibited provocative garb of any kind and, in particular, pants for women; it also required ties, suits, or sport jackets for men. A badboy/-girl look never got onto the show—except on performers. Although the rules were relaxed in the late sixties, decorum generally prevailed, and males

MICHAEL OCHS ARCHIVES, VENICE, CALIFORNIA

Jimmy Clanton, 1958

wore conservative ties, white shirts, with the option of an additional v-neck or crew-neck sweater. Footwear consisted of conventional wing-tip, oxford, or penny-loafer shoes—the early sixties featured white bucks and Hush Puppies—although baggy pleated pants and big-shouldered tweed or shiny sharkskin jackets echoed the dress of entertainers from the swing era of the 1940s. On special occasions, the boys might wear shawl-collared dinner jackets, which were often pastel or plaid with black lapels. Only the slicked-back Brylcreemed hair done in a DA (duck's ass) with a pompadour roll in front hinted at the bad-boy model. Crewcuts were scarce. Girls favored wool, angora, cotton blend, or synthetic sweaters with detachable collars of rabbit fur, velvet, or satin; or white Peter Pan collars and straight, circle, or bouffant skirts with hems well below the kneecaps. Often parochial school uniforms were covered up by the sweaters, uniform collars just peeking out. Pixie cuts, pony tails, and modest teased flip-up hairstyles gave way to the 1958 roller-set pageboy cut. At this time, too, bobby socks were replaced by colored tights, and show regular Carol Scaldeferri started a national fad for headbands.

In England, working-class "Teddy Boys" were much tougher in their adoption of the American film image of rockers, a look that Iain Chambers (in his book *Urban Rhythms*) claims set a working-class style of urban male elegance purposefully counter to the "straight adult world." In 1954 the notion of separate clothes for rock fans established the first link between rock music and counterculture styles, even though the fad for drape jackets with velvet collars, "brothel creepers" (thick-crepe-soled shoes), and pegged "drain pipe" pants had waned by the time that rock 'n' roll became widely popular.

American teens took longer to differentiate their images from those of adults. They started in

Hair braids and "xtensions" styled by Adriana Barrett, 1986, and extreme variation on the pompadour, ca. 1985 (John Sex at New York's Limelight Club)

GIRL LOVES BOY

VINNIE ZUFFANTE/STAR FILE

1962, but even then the fashion wasn't based primarily on the costume of performers. "Bandstand" rules relaxed to permit stretch pants with stirrups, culottes, clam diggers, and pedal pushers for women—as well as close-fitting sheath dresses. Male body-consciousness also emerged, reflected in narrower, sleeker jackets. By 1962, many females adopted the bad-girl hairstyle of the beehive teased and sprayed into extreme heights—to the annoyance of schoolteachers, who claimed that such hairy shapes blocked the view of students who had to sit behind them in class. Good-girl alternatives were still available as well, including the French twist and the bouffant flip, with hair turned up at the bottom, away from the face, in winglike projections. Some popular women performers such as the Ronettes and Supremes had similar bad- and good-girl hairdos.

About this time the surfing and folk music movements in their most popular manifestations—the Beach Boys and folkies Peter, Paul, and Mary, as well as the Kingston Trio—gave birth to a clean-cut collegiate sportswear image, with khaki pants, white Levi's, tennis shoes and loafers, and striped and plain ivy-league shirts. Hollywood films, which had been devouring the West Coast surf scene in a series of adolescent beach blanket fantasies (such as *Gidget*, with Sandra Dee in 1959, and the Frankie Avalon–Annette Funicello films, including *Beach Party* of 1963), promoted the fad for wetsuits, bikinis, and surf gear. A comparative minority of

Shag cut: Blackie Lawless of W.A.S.P., 1985. Flat top: Brian Drumm's flat topper comb with built-in spirit level

teen- and college-age women were influenced in 1963–64 by proto-hippie Joan Baez, who had long, loosely hanging hair, wore shapeless dresses or ultra-plain blouses and skirts, no make-up, and either sandals or no shoes at all. Bob Dylan also popularized blue chambray workshirts for undergraduate "intellectuals." Not until it became folk rock after 1965, did fans and singers adopt more obviously counterculture emblems of West Coast pastoral life, such as Indian cotton shirts and tunics and hair even longer than the Beatles'.

It was the Beatles who, in 1964, changed the look of popular music as well as its relation to fashion and even to high culture. The group not only disseminated the British Mod style worldwide, it also repudiated the hard-rock look of anti-fashion. Abandoning black leather jackets and tight jeans meant discarding the mythic aura of past rock gods for the glorification of the present singers and the promise of a new age. Moreover, the Beatles also changed their own images from year to year—beginning with the identical Cardin-like suits, moving toward a more romantic Mod sportswear look, and finally to outright hippiedom, complete with beards. The triumph of the Beatles was also simultaneous with the beginnings of designer fashion related to rock 'n' roll—designs meant for the majority, and not just for urban aficionados of the style.

Aside from the length of their bangs, the Beatles, with their neat tailored clothes and polite manners, were the answer to parental prayers for visual role models. But since the group was exclusively male, girls sought their models in the Fab Four's girlfriends, who wore Mary Quant "little girl"

miniskirts, which were styled just for teens and were not versions of adult clothes. By contrast, Courrèges's geometric, space-age-look miniskirt outfits were directed at an older, more affluent customer. However, both versions of the fashion made their wearers look presexual.

Although the Who was America's model for what British Mods looked like, the band was not in fact Mod. As the 1986 film *Absolute Beginners* showed, Mods between 1963 and 1966 wore such benign separates as anglicized adaptations of French, Italian, and American suits, sport parkas, and Fred Perry shirts. Their hair was short and neat, and they drove Vespa scooters. Beginning in 1963, the belated British television equivalent of "American Bandstand," "Juke Box Jury" advertised bright Carnaby Street fashions. One did not have to be under thirty to adopt such fashions. Wide lapels, flaring-bottomed trousers, bright shirts and ties, and hair down to the collar appeared on businessmen, and miniskirts adorned many women who no longer had the vintage thighs to wear them flatteringly.

The next development, American West Coast psychedelia, appealed to a more hard-core counterculture, for it was vernacular in origin, primitivizing in its throwback to rural handcrafted cultures, both in imagery and in decorative embellishment. It was offensive to the Establishment's esteem of neatness, which was associated with order. Inseparable from the music and drug culture beginning in 1966 until the end of the decade, psychedelic fashion with its tie-dying of t-shirts, hand appliquéing of denim separates, and patchwork quilting of dresses and shirts, was not a promising direction for the domestic mass-manufactured garments industry because of the large degree of hand labor involved. Instead, granny-dresses, peasant blouses, and unisex tunics and caftans of cotton poured in from India and the Orient, where hand labor was plentiful and cheap.

In England, as the psychedelic era burned itself out toward the end of the sixties, the skinhead proletariat look, with boots and braces, appeared as a backlash against what was perceived as the wimpy, androgynous, liberal, hypocritical, and spaced-out lethargy of hippies. The 1971 science-fiction film *Clockwork Orange* featured as hero (or antihero) a teenage British thug named Alex and his "Droogs"—pidgin Russian for pals, but it might have meant, in context, punks. The film formulated a generalized punk look before Vivienne Westwood and Malcolm McLaren began their punk collaboration in 1972.

Meanwhile, the British glitter rock of David Bowie in 1972 and 1973 influenced some British but very few American teens. Androgyny was acceptable for females, but it wouldn't do for young males unsure of their sexual identity. What united the otherwise disparate look of *Clockwork Orange* and David Bowie was, once again, science fiction. Ziggy Stardust after all was an outerspace alien, backed by his spiders from Mars. American disco fashion, circa 1974–75, also had a futuristic look, with its glossy space-age Spandex tops and "twirl" dance skirts, flared to move away from the body when women spun. Then there were the patterned leotard stockings worn with ultra-short "hot pants" and boots, and bell-bottoms stuffed into boots in the manner of a space uniform.

Whereas the disco look was the mainstream music image, Vivienne Westwood sought the confrontational antithesis when she dressed the Sex Pistols from 1975 to 1978. She tried to make them as controversial as possible. She told *GQ* in January 1983: "We were especially concerned with the clothes' sexuality, of course, because that's what made them subversive. . . . The look evolved from sex and bondage gear but was more street-oriented. Evidently the time was ripe for zippers, slogans and ripped T-shirts, and that's essentially how Punk dressing was born." When asked if she thought of herself as a designer of unisex clothes, she replied "it's all gesture and attitude anyway, so I guess I'm in favor of creating unisex looks." Malcolm McLaren told Krystina Kitsis in *ZG Magazine* (April 1982) that McLaren-Westwood fashions had to do with glamour as well as subversion: "From some people's viewpoint, being glamorous is very much a part of appealing to the status quo; but for others, being most unappealing is glamorous."

In 1977 Zandra Rhodes redesigned the punk image into the type of glamour McLaren opposed. She called it "Conceptual Chic" and claimed (in the *Art of Zandra Rhodes*), that a 1938 Schiaparelli dress, with a Salvador Dali print pattern depicting fabric tears, influenced her artfully and precisely shaped holes, edge-stitched and pinned with silver safety pins, while the rest of these perforated dresses were decorated with rhinestones and tiny seed pearls. Unlike the work of Westwood and McLaren, Rhodes's figure-revealing evening gowns were sexually attractive in the conventional sense and also luxurious.

Her use of satin, loops of silver for chains and pins, and silk jersey sharply contrasted with the punk Roxy Club costume of torn rubber t-shirts with holes, black plastic garbage bags secured with safety pins as tunics and dresses, and laddered stockings. Rhodes also cited the influence of the science-fiction film *Star Wars* on her textile prints at the end of 1977.

Meanwhile, Westwood continued to use what she called the "technique of keeping something modern while establishing symbolic connections with the past" (*Harpers and Queen*, April 1983). In dressing Adam and the Ants and Bow Wow Wow from 1980 to 1982, she and Malcolm McLaren had recourse to adventure stories of the past. Such historical reference was not in itself new to fashion design but what was striking was their choice of pop cartoon references: "All of my sources, the pirates and the Indians, are like comic book characters that appeal to the emotions," Westwood told the *Soho News* in October 1981. Her 1982 Buffalo Gals line paralleled the release of McLaren's *Duck Rock* album, which featured musical appropriations from American square-dance songs. Her pirate look, which used deliberately coarse fabric and loose, tied-on, wraparound drapery, prefigures the 1982–83 Japanese fashion coup d'état, which would use the same technique, but with more abstract imagery and without reference to rock, youth culture, or specific quasi-historical parables. Rei Kawakubo even appropriated the torn holes in her 1983 collection, which alluded to concepts in 1977 British punk fashion. Issey Miyake was reported to have attended Westwood's showings, and his 1984 line showed great affinity for Westwood's use of Third World sources. New York East Village bohemian outfits from 1984 through 1986 combined the punk and Japanese sources, with an emphasis on 1960s hand-crafting, including fabric painting, multi-

*B*etsey Johnson

plication of pattern pieces, and ornamentation. A style unsuited to profitable mass production, these American versions lost their connection with democratic rock-related garments and aligned themselves with the local art gallery scene.

More promising directions for the alliance of fashion and music culture have been shown by the Americans Stephen Sprouse and Betsey Johnson,

who couple contemporary production technology with rock-music imagery. Sprouse, who designed for Deborah Harry of Blondie, became the young star of the American fashion scene from 1983 to 1985, with his simply cut tunic mini-dresses in day-glo colors, graffiti-printed tights, velvet blazers, and bell-bottomed pants, all with overtones of the 1960s. However, his use of expensive fabrics, plus coat and jacket patterns that required expert tailoring, raised retail prices beyond the means of his biggest potential market—rock fans. Nevertheless, as *New York Times* fashion writer John Duka pointed out in an August 21, 1984 article, "they are the first clothes in years to tap into the currents of popular culture and to translate the drive of rock music and MTV videos into retail form."

Betsey Johnson's sportswear doubles as evening wear because of its high-impact colors and contrasts, body-fitting cuts, and imagery drawn from modern dance and rock music. Working in knit fabrics and designs that require no hand tailoring holds down the cost of production, although prices for her limited editions still hover above those of the mass market. Most of her clothes are sold through upscale mail-order catalogs or in her own boutiques; they are often too assertive for conservative department-store buyers.

Johnson's twenty years of experience in designing for rock musicians as well as for the fashion market has afforded her an overview of the relationship between the two realms. She prefers fash-

*B*etsey Johnson: from the 1986 collection; sketch from the 1960s; and contemporary promotional postcard

ion design, because it demands less self-effacement as an artist:

I think designing for rock people is costume designing. Although it's more fun, much more exciting than designing for yourself—what I do here—it's also very time-consuming and a one-to-one relationship.

I love production and just can't do a lot of custom work. I don't just want to be a dressmaker, although I love costume design and would like to dress an orchestra or an opera.

Nevertheless, she is currently designing the Bangles' new look, a collaboration she feels will be successful because of the singers' affinity with her work. Ordinarily, custom designing is less comfortable for her because her fashion collections express her own definite personality. When someone with a personal affinity for that character sees her style, they buy her garments. When she designs for rock groups, she must subordinate her signature look to their image requirements.

Johnson feels that music television has profoundly influenced the American fashion industry by putting it into an "overlap phase," in which all the style cycles are layered on top of each other from different years: "You used to think that a trend lasted this long, and now a trend is popular for thirty seconds. Instead of people going through one at a time, they can go through five in a day: wearing one to the office, another funky thing after work, and end up at the Palladium in something completely different from the three earlier outfits. I like doing collections that have everything in them. I finally understand that, and my customers always understand that." She says that although MTV is a great boon to her business, the masses don't want to look as sexy as Madonna. "It's what you take from it. Every kid can get a black t-shirt and cut it off short or cut off the armholes and get another lace t-shirt underneath. The idea is for everyone. You can take the sexiest of how Prince looks and make some element of it work. I think he's doing wonders for cropped tops. That's the new bra, and it's the best-selling item in our new store." Johnson attributes the cropped-top look to Prince more than to Madonna, because Madonna's first impact was the bra straps and bra showing, but she feels we notice stomachs more on boys. However, she felt Madonna's Marilyn Monroe *How to Marry a Millionaire* sexy look for the video "Material Girl" was popular but was less successful as a style for a rock star because it was impossible for most wanna-be fans to copy. One needed a professional dressmaker to fabricate the Hollywood movie star gown.

Pop music, usually marketed as MOR (Middle of the Road) or AOR (Adult Oriented Rock) on soft-rock radio stations, often incorporates both Hollywood star glamour and fashion dressing that reinforces specific trends. Bob Mackie designs for film (for example, *Lady Sings the Blues* [with Ray Agahayan]), starring Diana Ross in 1972, and *Brenda Starr*, starring Brooke Shields in 1986, for stage and television singers, and for his own fashion line. He believes that performers make an impact on fashion when they perform *as themselves* rather than as fictionalized characters. He cited Cher's late-

*N*ight School: A Performance Designed to Teach You a Lesson. *Written, produced, and directed by Francine Hunter of Jungle Red Studios and staged at the Mudd Club, April 1979.*

jungle red

presents

NIGHT SCHOOL

sixties look (before he worked with her) as a prime inspiration for "anti-fashion fashion": she was the first pop/rock singer to have long straight hair, bell-bottomed pants, and a t-shirt. Mackie sees Madonna's outerwear-underwear look as the final popular focus of an image that had been evolving for some time.

Mackie believes that MTV has made the rock 'n' roll people start dressing up more than they formerly did. For him, it has brought fashion and

costume closer together. Asked if any of the ideas that he used for performers have translated directly into his own collections, he replies that he doesn't think of them as separate, that the performers' outfits are magnified versions of fashion. But, as with Betsey Johnson, Mackie's fashion is not middle-of-the-road sportswear; it's luxurious beaded gowns, elegant suits and furs for women who want to stand out in a crowd. Mackie recalled (in a 1986 talk at the Fashion Institute of Technology) that when he was about to start his fashion business on Seventh Avenue in New York, he was cautioned that "women don't want to look like stars." "Don't believe it," he told his audience.

Larry LeGaspi, another rock and pop costume designer, also creates fashion within the glamour realm. He feels that MTV has been a force in getting the audiences to dress up more, and it has increased the artist's business. LeGaspi has taken the elements of his earlier rock costumes, the heavy-metal studs and trapunto detailing, and combined them with soft draping fabric to create romantic gowns and dresses rather than tough or hard-edged images. Both Whitney Houston and Dionne Warwick have bought his creations recently. His science-fiction imagery of the seventies has been sublimated into the realm of the Great Goddess.

While high fashion may appropriate elements of the bad-girl rock style—such as tight fit, short skirts, an emphasis on silhouette and high contrast of dark and light and colors—the working-

Richard Erker: Lion's claw rings, 1972, made for Paul Stanley of Kiss, and boots fashioned for Billy Idol, 1986

RINGS PHOTO: JOHN BASCARINO BOOTS PHOTO: RICHARD ERKER COURTESY RICHARD ERKER

class and mass-produced aesthetic of the genre is at odds with American signature designer sportswear that trades in the Seventh Avenue rhetoric of "sporting splendor" and "striking a balance of grace and grandeur." Nevertheless, the hand-crafted personalization of dressmaker skills used in glitter rock and glamour pop makes wide distribution of that style economically unfeasible. Moreover, department store retail chains generally avoid stocking very provocative designs; their attempt is to appeal to the greatest number of customers—whose taste is generally middle of the road. The person who wants fashion that really looks like rock or pop star material must go to a specialty store. For this reason, some of the fashion designers who deal in explicitly sexy imagery and knit-to-closely-fit fabrication techniques—like Betsey Johnson with rock music and dance imagery, and Norma Kamali with Hollywood film inspiration—have their own outlets or sell directly to boutiques and mail-order houses. Their examples show how it is possible to turn the science-fiction theme of the taming of nature (and thus sexuality) into its opposing mythology, which proclaims the vitality of the ancient Great Goddess. The mythic appeal of archetypal imagery allows clothing designers to bridge the gap between high fashion and low popular-culture romance, between the good virgin androgyne and the sexy bad-girl rebel of rock.

If signature fashion is to embrace rock culture and costume intimately, the most advanced fabric and fiber developments and construction procedures, as well as innovation in simplifying pattern design, will have to be used to create inexpensive, and therefore democratically available, mythically potent images anchored in the ancient past. Video (which Kamali was one of the earliest designers to use) or computers will model designs—serving, perhaps, as the fashion magazines of the future. Rock 'n' roll music has never been shy about appropriating the newest technology. If fashion is to participate fully in this realm, it must do the same.

Bibliography

The following works were invaluable as secondary sources for *Getting It On*.

Abrams, M. H. (1971) *Natural Supernaturalism: Tradition and Revolution in Romantic Literature*, W. W. Norton, New York.

Alain (Emile-Auguste Chartier). (1973) *The Gods*, New Directions Paperback, New York.

Anson, Robert. (1981) *Gone Crazy and Back Again: The Rise and Fall of the Rolling Stone Generation*, Doubleday, Garden City, New York.

Ashton, Dore. (1980) *A Fable of Modern Art*, Thames and Hudson, New York.

Bangs, Lester. (1980) "Heavy Metal," and "Protopunk: The Garage Bands," *Rolling Stone Illustrated History of Rock and Roll*, Random House, New York.

Barthes, Roland. (1983) *The Fashion System*, Hill and Wang, New York.

———. (1977) *Image–Music–Text*, Hill and Wang, New York.

———. (1972) *Mythologies*, Hill and Wang, New York.

Bashe, Philip. (1985) *Heavy Metal Thunder*, Doubleday, Garden City, New York.

Beltz, Carl. (1969) *The Story of Rock*, Harper Colophon, New York.

Bergman, Billy. (1985) *Goodtime Kings: Emerging African Pop*, William Morrow, New York.

———, and Richard Horn. (1985) *Recombinant Do-Re-Mi: Frontiers of the Rock Era*, William Morrow, New York.

Breskin, David. (1982) "Talking Heads," *The Year in Rock 1981–82*, Putnam, New York.

Brosnan, John. (1978) *Future Tense: The Cinema of Science Fiction*, St. Martin's Press, New York.

Burroughs, William S. (1966) *Naked Lunch*, Grove Press, New York.

———. (1964) *Nova Express*, 1980 Collection, Grove Press, New York.

———. (1980) *Port of Saints*, Blue Wind Press, Berkeley, California.

———. (1969, 1980) *The Wild Boys*, Grove Press, New York.

Busner, Gene. (1985) *The Rhythm and Blues Story*, Julian Messner, New York.

Campbell, Joseph. (1969) *Flight of the Wild Gander*, Viking Press, New York.

———. (1949) *Hero with a Thousand Faces*, Princeton University Press, Princeton.

———. (1970) *The Masks of God: Creative Mythology*, Viking Press, New York.

———. (1972) *Myths to Live By*, Viking Press, New York.

Campbell, Joseph, editor. (1970) *Myths, Dreams, and Religion*, Viking Press, New York.

Carlson, Peter. (September 1983) "London's Designers Alter the Shape of Fashion," *GQ*.

———. (October 1977) "Portrait in Black: Is There Life After Punk?" *GQ*.

———. (January 1983) "Vivienne Westwood: Shock Treatments," *GQ*.

Carr, Roy, and Mick Farren. (1982) *Elvis Presley: The Illustrated Record*, Crown, New York.

Carson, Tom. (1980) "David Bowie," *Rolling Stone Illustrated History of Rock and Roll*, Random House, New York.

Chambers, Iain. (1985) *Urban Rhythms: Pop Music and Popular Culture*, St. Martin's Press, New York.

Chierichetti, David. (1976) *Hollywood Costume Design*, Harmony Books, New York.

Clark, Dick. (1981) *Dick Clark's The First 25 Years of Rock and Roll*, Greenwich House, New York.

Colles, Ted, and Paul Foss. (Winter 1983) "Demolition Man," *Art & Text*, no. 10.

Consodine, J. D. (1982) "A.O.R. Rock," *The Year in Rock 1981–82*, Putnam, New York.

Cott, Jonathan. (1980) "Buddy Holly and the Crickets," *Rolling Stone Illustrated History of Rock and Roll*, Random House, New York.

————. (1985) *Dylan*, Dolphin/Doubleday, Garden City, New York.

Coupe, Stuart, and Glenn Baker. (1983) *The New Rock 'n' Roll: The A–Z of Rock in the '80s*, St. Martin's Press, New York.

Couperie, Pierre, and others. (1968) *A History of the Comic Strip*, Crown, New York.

Crocker, Chris. (1985) *Cyndi Lauper*, Julian Messner, New York.

Darter, Tom (compiler). (1984) *The Art of Electronic Music*, Quill, New York.

Duka, John. (August 28, 1984) "The Rock Connection," *New York Times Magazine*.

Duncan, Robert. (1984) *The Noise: Notes from a Rock 'n' Roll Era*, Ticknor and Fields, New York.

Eliade, Mircea. (1960) *Myths, Dreams and Mysteries: An Encounter Between Contemporary Faith and Archaic Realities*, Harper Torchbook, New York.

Emerson, Ken. (1980) "Britain: The Second Wave," *Rolling Stone Illustrated History of Rock and Roll*, Random House, New York.

————. (May 5, 1985) "David Byrne—Thinking Man's Rock Star," *New York Times Magazine*.

Errigo, Angie, and Steve Leaning. (1979) *Rock Album Art*, Octopus/Mayflower, London.

Farren, Mick. (1985) *The Black Leather Jacket*, Abbeville Press, New York.

Feuer, Jane. (1982) *The Hollywood Musical*, Indiana University Press, Bloomington.

Flans, Robyn. (1983) *From Rock to New Wave*, Sharon Publications, Cresskill, New York.

Frazer, Sir James G. (1922) *The Golden Bough: A Study in Magic and Religion*, vol. 1, Macmillan, New York, abridged edition.

Frith, Simon. (1981) *Sound Effects: Youth, Leisure, and the Politics of Rock 'n' Roll*, Pantheon, New York.

Fulpen, H. V. (1982) *The Beatles: An Illustrated Diary*, Putnam, New York.

Gerberg, Mort. (1983) *The Arbor House Book of Cartooning*, Arbor House, New York.

Gilbert, Douglas. (1940, 1968) *American Vaudeville: Its Life and Times*, Dover, New York.

Gill, Anton. (1984) *Mad About the Boy: The Life and Times of Boy George and Culture Club*, Holt, Rinehart and Winston, New York.

Gillette, Charlie. (1970, 1983) *The Sound of the City: The Rise of Rock and Roll*, Pantheon, New York.

Gilmore, Mikal, and Spottswood Erwing. (1982) "Brian Eno," *The Year in Rock 1981–82*, Putnam, New York.

Goldman, Albert. (1981) *Elvis*, McGraw-Hill, New York.

Graves, Robert. (1966) *The Greek Myths*, vol. 1, Penguin Books, Middlesex, England.

————. (1964) *Hebrew Myths*, Doubleday, Garden City, New York.

————. (1948) *The White Goddess*, Farrar, Straus & Giroux, New York.

Guralnick, Peter. (1980) "Elvis Presley" and "Rockabilly," *Rolling Stone Illustrated History of Rock and Roll*, Random House, New York.

Hammond, Harry, and Gered Mankowitz. (1984) *Pop Shots: A 35-Year Perspective of Music Performers Through the Photography of Harry Hammond and Gered Mankowitz*, Harper and Row, New York.

Hansen, Barry. (1980) "Doo-Wop," *Rolling Stone Illustrated History of Rock and Roll*, Random House, New York.

Hendler, Herb. (1983) *Year by Year in the Rock Era: Events and Conditions Shaping the Rock Generations That Reshaped America*, Greenwood Press, Westport, Connecticut, and London, England.

Herring, Peter. (1984) *Rock Giants*, W. H. Smith, New York.

Hibbard, Don J., and Carol Kaleialoha. (1983) *The Role of Rock: A Guide to the Social and Political Consequences of Rock Music*, Prentice-Hall, Englewood Cliffs, New Jersey.

Highwater, Jamake. (1984) *Ritual of the Wind: North American Indian Ceremonies, Music, and Dance*, Alfred Van Der Mark, New York.

Hirshey, Gerri. (1984) *Nowhere to Run: The Story of Soul Music*, Times Books, New York.

Hofmann, Werner. (1957) *Caricature: From Leonardo to Picasso*, Crown, New York.

Hoggard, Stuart. (1980) *David Bowie Changes: An Illustrated Biography*, Omnibus Press, London.

Hopkins, Jerry. (1985) *Bowie*, Macmillan, New York.

———. (1981) *Elvis, the Final Years*, Berkeley Books, New York.

Ivory, Steven. (1985) *Tina*, Putnam, New York.

Jameson, Fredric. (1981) *The Political Unconscious: Narrative as a Socially Symbolic Act*, Cornell University Press, Ithaca, New York.

Jones, Dylan. (March 1986) "Lydon on Lager," *I-D Magazine*, London.

Jung, C. G. (1938) *The Basic Writings of C. G. Jung*, Modern Library, New York.

———. (1957) *The Undiscovered Self*, Little, Brown, and Company, Boston.

Keil, Charles. (1966) *Urban Blues*, University of Chicago Press, Chicago.

Kitsis, Krystina. (April 1982) "Malcolm McLaren," *Z.G.*, no. 7, London.

Klinkowitz, Jerome. (1980) *The American 1960s: Imaginative Acts in a Decade of Change*, Iowa State University Press, Ames, Iowa.

Korner, Anthony. (Summer 1986) "Aurora Musicalis," *Artforum*, no. 10, New York.

Laver, James. (1964) *Costume in the Theatre*, Farrar, Straus & Giroux, New York.

Lee-Potter, Charlie. (1984) *Sportswear in Vogue Since 1910*, Abbeville Press, New York.

Legett, Carol. (1985) *The Heavy Metal Bible*, Pinnacle Books, New York.

Levi-Strauss, Claude. (1981) *The Naked Man: Introduction to a Science of Mythology*, vol. 4, Harper & Row, Cambridge, Massachusetts.

Logan, Nick, and Bob Woffinden. (1977) *The Illustrated Encyclopedia of Rock*, Harmony Books, New York.

Mackie, Bob. (1979) *Dressing for Glamour*, A & W Publishers, New York.

Malinowski, Bronislaw. (1954) *Magic, Science and Religion*, Doubleday, Garden City, New York.

Malone, Bill. (1985) *Country Music U.S.A.*, University of Texas Press, Austin.

Marcus, Greil. (1975) *Mystery Train: Images of America in Rock 'n' Roll Music*, Dutton, New York.

Marranca, Bonnie. (1984) *Theatrewritings*, Performing Arts Journal Publications, New York.

Marsh, Dave, and others, editors. (1985) *The First Rock and Roll Confidential Report*, Random House, New York.

Marsh, Dave. (1985) *Fortunate Son: The Best of Dave Marsh*, Random House, New York.

———. (1980) "The Who," *Rolling Stone Illustrated History of Rock and Roll*, Random House, New York.

McConathy, Dave, with Diana Vreeland. (1976) *Hollywood Costume*, Harry N. Abrams and the Metropolitan Museum of Art, New York.

McGill, Leonard. (1980) *Disco Dressing*, Prentice-Hall, Englewood Cliffs, New Jersey.

McLaren, Malcolm. (1986) "Mile High Club," *File #25/Art & Text #22* (joint issue), Melbourne, Australia.

Mellers, Wilfrid. (1985) *A Darker Shade of Pale: A Backdrop to Bob Dylan*, Faber and Faber, Ltd., London.

Mercatante, Anthony. (1978) *Good and Evil: Mythology and Folklore*, Harper & Row, New York.

Miller, David. (1970) "Orestes: Myth and Dream as Catharsis," *Myths, Dreams and Religion*, Dutton, New York.

Miller, Jim, editor. (1980) *Rolling Stone Illustrated History of Rock and Roll*, Random House, New York.

Mills, Bart. (1985) *Tina*, Warner Books, New York.

Obrecht, Jas, editor. (1984) *Masters of Heavy Metal*, Quill/A Guitar Player Book, New York.

Palmer, Robert. (1980) "Rock Begins" and "Jazz Rock," *Rolling Stone Illustrated History of Rock and Roll*, Random House, New York.

Palmer, Tony. (1976) *All You Need Is Love: The Story of Popular Music*, Viking Press, New York.

Parry, Albert. (1971) *Tattoo*, Macmillan, New York.

Pascall, Jeremy. (1984) *The Illustrated History of Rock Music*, Simon & Schuster, New York.

Phillips, John A. (1984) *Eve: The History of an Idea*, Harper & Row, New York.

Piccarella, John. (1982) "Post-Punk British Rock," *The Year in Rock 1981–82*, Putnam, New York.

Pollock, Bruce. (1983) *When the Music Matttered: Rock in the 1960s*, Holt, Rinehart and Winston, New York.

Powell, Fiona Russell. (1985) "London," *Fashion 85*, St. Martin's Press, New York.

Price, Steven. (1974) *Take Me Home: The Rise of Country and Western Music*, Praeger, New York.

Pullar, Philippa. (1970) *Consuming Passions: Being an Historical Inquiry into Certain English Appetites*, Little, Brown and Company, Toronto, Canada.

Raso, Anne M. (June 1986) "Sigue Sigue Sputnik: Swindlers or Stars," *Pulse*.

Robinson, Lisa. (September 1986) "Material Boys: Sigue Sigue Sputnik Sells Space," *Vogue*.

Rockwell, John. (1983) *All American Music: Composition in the Late Twentieth Century*, Knopf, New York.

————. (1980) "Art Rock" and "The Sound of Manhattan," *Rolling Stone Illustrated History of Rock and Roll*, Random House, New York.

————. (July 27, 1986) "Where Avant-Garde Meets Rock and Roll, Music Flourishes," *New York Times*.

Roxon, Lillian. (1969) *Roxon's Rock Encyclopedia*, Grosset and Dunlap, New York.

Russell, Ethan. (1985) *Dear Mr. Fantasy: Diary of a Decade*, Houghton Mifflin, Boston.

Salzman, Eric. (1975) *Twentieth-Century Music: An Introduction*, Prentice-Hall, Englewood Cliffs, New Jersey.

Savage, Jon. (October 1983) "Guerilla Graphics: The Tactics of Agit-Pop Art," *The Face*.

Schickel, Richard. (1968) *The Disney Version: The Life, Times, Art and Commerce of Walt Disney*, Simon & Schuster, New York.

Scholes, Robert, and Eric S. Rabkin. (1978) *Science Fiction: History, Science, Vision*, Oxford University Press, Oxford, England.

Scully, Vincent. (1979) *The Earth, the Temple, and the Gods: Greek Sacred Architecture*, Yale University Press, New Haven, revised edition.

Shore, Michael, with Dick Clark. (1985) *The History of American Bandstand*, Random House, New York.

Simonton, Thomas, and Baldwin Ward, editors. (1960) *Historic Decade 1950–1960*, Year and News Front, New York.

Smucker, Tom. (1980) "Disco," *Rolling Stone Illustrated History of Rock and Roll*, Random House, New York.

Sobchack, Vivian. (1985) "The Virginity of the Astronauts," *Shadows of the Magic Lamp: Fantasy and Science Fiction in Film*, Southern Illinois University Press, Carbondale and Edwardsville.

Suares, Jean-Claude, Richard Siegel, and David Owen. (1979) *Fantastic Planets*, Addison House, Danbury, Connecticut.

Taraborelli, J. Randy, with Reginald Wilson and Daryl Minger. (1985) *Diana*, Doubleday, Garden City, New York.

Taylor, Paul. (April 1986) "Malcolm McLaren: Pop's Smoking Pistol," *Vogue*.

Testa, Burt. (1982) "New Wave," *The Year in Rock 1981–82*, G. P. Putnam, New York.

Toll, Robert C. (1974) *Blacking Up: The Minstrel Show in Nineteenth Century America*, Oxford University Press, Oxford, England.

Toop, David. (1984) *The Rap Attack: African Jive to New York Hip Hop*, South End Press, Boston.

Tosches, Nick. (1982) *Hellfire: The Jerry Lee Lewis Story*, Dell, New York.

Unger, Roberto Mangabeira. (1984) *Passion: An Essay on Personality*, Macmillan, New York.

Van der Horst, Brian. (1973) *Rock Music*, Franklin Watts, New York.

Vare, Ethlie Ann, and Ed Ochs. (1984) *Stevie Nicks*, Ballantine Books, New York.

Waller, Don. (1985) *The Motown Story*, Charles Scribner's Sons, New York.

Willis, Ellen. (1980) "Janice Joplin," *Rolling Stone Illustrated History of Rock and Roll*, Random House, New York.

White, Charles. (1984) *The Life and Times of Little Richard*, Harmony Books, New York.

Zolla, Elemire. (1981) *Archetypes: The Persistence of Unifying Patterns*, Harcourt Brace Jovanovich, New York.

Acknowledgments

I would like to thank Hap Hatton, Paul Taylor,

and my editor Alan Axelrod for their criticisms and suggestions,

my agent Barbara Kouts for her encouragement,

and Ellen Colón-Lugo for her photo research.

Much of this book was also made possible through interviews

and information generously supplied by individuals

to whom I wish to express my appreciation,

especially to Larry LeGaspi, Bob Mackie, Betsey Johnson,

Fleur Thiemeyer, Cecil Gorey, Ray Brown, Glen Palmer,

Zario of "After Six," Roberta Brooks, Josh Baer, and Tim Grajek.

Music photographer and photo archivist David Redfern

provided many classic images.   Above all, I am grateful to all the

photographers whose names are given throughout this book

and to G. E. Smith, who inspired the idea for *Getting It On*

with conversation about his performance outfits.

Index